TUDOR
BOOK OF DAYS

This book belongs to:

_____

_____

_____

TUDOR ✖ TIMES

Books of Hours

During the late Middle Ages and Renaissance period, one of the most coveted items a literate person could own was a Book of Hours.

Books of Hours were designed to aid lay people in the practice of their religion, by collecting biblical texts, prayers and elements of the liturgy for them to read throughout the day, emulating the 'Hours' or regular services of the religious life.

Members of religious orders repeated the Divine Office, divided into seven canonical Hours each day, beginning with the combined Hours of Matins and Lauds, recited between midnight and dawn, then at three hourly intervals, Prime, Tierce, Sext and None, with the final Hours of Vespers and Compline in the evening. Time-keeping was more fluid then than it is now, and the recitation of the Hours would vary with the seasons and the light.

From the eleventh century, the Little Office of the Blessed Virgin Mary was added to the canonical Hours. This was taken up with enthusiasm by the laity as the cult of the Virgin became an enduring part of popular devotion and the Books of Hours commissioned over the succeeding centuries had the Little Office at their heart.

Each Book of Hours had three elements: the essential, the secondary, and the accessory. The essential consisted of the perpetual calendar, showing the fixed and moveable feast days and saints days – the most widely venerated saints would be listed, together with saints popular in the region the Book was created, or especially meaningful to the owner. Customarily, the major feast days in each month would be marked with gold or red lettering. The calendar was numbered, not with the days of the month in consecutive numbering as is the modern practice, but by reference to the 'kalends' or first of the month; the 'nones' (the fifth or seventh of the month) and the 'ides' (the thirteenth or fifteenth). The calendar also showed the 'golden number', used to calculate Easter.

Generally, each month covered the right-hand-side of the open book (the recto) and the left-hand-side of the following page (verso). The month pages were decorated with activities suitable for the month – harvesting in June, ploughing in October, for example, or the zodiac sign.

Following the calendar, came the Little Office, the Penitential Psalms, the Litany, the Office of the Dead and the Suffrages of the Saints.

The secondary portion contained passages from the Gospels of Matthew, Mark, Luke and John which refer to the coming of Christ, followed by the Passion as described in John. There were then additional prayers to the Virgin, and other Offices, such as that of the Hours of the Cross or the Fifteen Joys of the Virgin, might follow. The final element, the accessory, contained more Psalms and prayers.

The popularity of Books of Hours

By the late fifteenth century, Books of Hours were so popular that centres such as Paris and Bruges produced them en masse. There were several stages to production – the acquisition of the vellum, the ruling of lines, the writing of the text, then the creation of the borders and ornamentation, before the final addition of the illustrations – called miniatures, regardless of size.

Higher up the social scale, Books of Hours were individually commissioned, frequently as a bride-gift from the husband for his new wife, and the level of decoration, the number of colours used in the illumination, and the quantity of gold, silver or expensive lapis blue used, depended on what the purchaser could afford. The Books were often personalised by the depiction of the owner and his or her family, coats-of-arms, and symbols relating to the individual. For example, the Book of Hours of Anne, Duchess of Brittany and Queen of France, shows Anne herself, together with her husband and children. Queen Anne paid 600 gold écus for its decoration.

The Books were further individualised by the owner writing notes in them, sometimes recording events – such as the birth of her granddaughter in 1489 by Lady Margaret Beaufort, mother of King Henry VII. Often, friends or lovers would write verses to each other, an example being a loving exchange between King Henry VIII and Anne Boleyn.

Books of Hours were prized possessions, handed down through the generations and often refurbished and recovered.

With the coming of the printing press, many Books of Hours were mass-produced and their popularity in this new format continued. In Protestant countries, which eschewed excessive devotion to the Virgin, they were superseded by prayer-books and family Bibles.

TUDOR BOOK OF DAYS

We cannot, alas, reproduce the extraordinary beauty of the original Books of Hours, but in the Tudor Book of Days, we have sought to combine some of the functions of the originals in an attractive contemporary format. Our Book of Days is a perpetual calendar, which allows you to enter the events most important to you, your friends and family, and preserve them indefinitely, untrammelled by the days of the week or the year.

We have preserved the traditional lists of feast and saints' days, and, for each day of the year, we have highlighted an interesting event that took place between around 1485 and 1625. The index at the back has a short entry on individuals and events.

Note on dates

Tudor and Renaissance dating practices differed from modern ones and can be confusing. In much of Europe, the year began on Easter Day, although in some countries (including England and Scotland) it began on Ladyday (25th March). In 1582, with the adoption of the Gregorian Calendar, which moved the calendar forward ten days, most of Europe began dating the year from 1st January, although that was not part of the papal bull implementing the changes to days. This is called New Style dating. Scotland adopted New Style for dating the year on 1st January 1599 Old Style, which became 1st January 1600 in New Style but did not change the days to the Gregorian pattern. England changed both in 1750.

Thus, the date in New Style of 14th March 1603, was 4th March 1602 in England, 4th March 1603 in Scotland, and 14th March 1603 in most of Europe. In common with usual practice, this book adopts New Style for years, whilst retaining the day and month used at the time in the relevant country.

Leap day was not 29th February, but was inserted between 24th and 25th February.

PERSONAL DETAILS

Name

Surname

Home address

Telephone

Mobile

E-mail

Date of birth

Place of birth

website

wifi

login

Home wifi

login

Family doctor	Dentist
Address	Address
Telephone	Telephone
Blood group	
Allergies	
Vaccinations	
Passport No	
Valid until	
Visa	
Expiry date	
Driving licence	
Expiry date	

YEAR PLANNER

January

_____
_____
_____
_____
_____
_____
_____
_____
_____

February

_____
_____
_____
_____
_____
_____
_____
_____
_____

March

_____
_____
_____
_____
_____
_____
_____
_____
_____

April

_____
_____
_____
_____
_____
_____
_____
_____
_____

May

_____
_____
_____
_____
_____
_____
_____
_____
_____

June

_____
_____
_____
_____
_____
_____
_____
_____
_____

July

August

September

October

November

December

MONTH PLANNER

January

1   Henry, Duke of Cornwall, was born (1511)

2   Lady Joan FitzGerald, Countess of Desmond, died (1565)

3   John Clerk, Bishop of Bath & Wells, died (1541)

4   Roger Ascham, scholar and tutor to Elizabeth I, was buried (1569)

5   Richard Wiles, geographer and poet, was born (1546)

6   King Henry VIII of England married Anne of Cleves, his fourth wife (1540)

7   Katharine of Aragon, Henry VIII's first wife, died (1536)

8   King James V of Scotland was buried at Holyrood Abbey (1543)

9   Clement Adams, school master and map engraver, died (1587)

10   Lady Penelope Devereux married Sir Richard Rich (1581)

11   Sir Richard Southwell, Privy Councillor and courtier, died (1564)

12   William Howard, 1st Baron Howard of Effingham, died (1573)

13   Edmund Spenser, poet, died (1599)

14   Francis Kett, physician, was burned for heresy (1589)

15   Elizabeth I was crowned Queen of England (1559)

16   Sir Anthony Denny, courtier and close friend of Henry VIII, was born (1501)

17   Henry Grey, Duke of Suffolk, was born (1517)

18   King Henry VII of England married Elizabeth of York (1486)

19   King François II of France was born (1544)

20   Miles Coverdale, Bishop of Exeter and Bible translator, died (1569)

21   First Parliament of King Henry VIII opened (1510)

22   John Donne, English poet, was born (1573)

23   William Baffin, English navigator and explorer, died (1622)

24   Foundation stone of Henry VII's Lady Chapel at Westminster Abbey was laid (1503)

25   Probable date of secret marriage of King Henry VIII to Anne Boleyn, his second wife (1533)

26   Thomas Howard, 4th Duke of Norfolk, degraded from Order of the Garter (1572)

27   Sir Francis Drake, courtier and explorer, died (1596)

28   King Henry VII of England was born (1457)

29   Sir Thomas Pope, founder of Trinity College, Oxford, died (1559)

30   Lady Anne Clifford, Countess of Dorset and Countess of Pembroke & Montgomery, was born (1590)

31   Guy Fawkes was executed for his role in the Gunpowder Plot (1606)

Birthdays	Anniversaries	Reminders	Projects

Gardening	Events	Occasions	Festivals

JANUARY

1   **Feast of the Circumcision**

Henry, Duke of Cornwall,
was born (1511)

2   **St Basil the Great's Day**

Lady Joan FitzGerald,
Countess of Desmond, died
(1565)

3   **St Genevieve of Paris' Day**

John Clerk, Bishop of Bath
& Wells, died (1541)

4 **Octave of the Holy Innocents**

Roger Ascham, scholar and tutor to Elizabeth I, was buried (1569)

5 **Twelfth Night**

Richard Wiles, geographer and poet, was born (1546)

6 **Feast of the Epiphany**

King Henry VIII of England married Anne of Cleves, his fourth wife (1540)

January

7   **St Cedd, Bishop of London's Day**

Katharine of Aragon, Henry VIII's first wife, died (1536)

8   **St Wulsin's Day**

King James V of Scotland was buried at Holyrood Abbey (1543)

9   Clement Adams, school master and map engraver, died (1587)

10 **St Geraint of Wales' Day**

Lady Penelope Devereux
married Sir Richard Rich
(1581)

11 **St Brandan's Day**

Sir Richard Southwell,
Privy Councillor and
courtier, died (1564)

12 William Howard, 1st Baron
Howard of Effingham,
died (1573)

13 **St Mungo of Scotland's Day**

Edmund Spenser, poet, died (1599)

14 **St Felix of Nola's Day**

Francis Kett, physician, was burned for heresy (1589)

15 **St Isisdore's Day**

Elizabeth I was crowned Queen of England (1559)

16 **St Marcellus' Day**

Sir Anthony Denny, courtier and close friend of Henry VIII, was born (1501)

17 **St Antony of Egypt's Day**

Henry Grey, Duke of Suffolk, was born (1517)

18 **St Prisca's Day**

King Henry VII of England married Elizabeth of York (1486)

19   St Wulfstan's Day

King François II of France
was born (1544)

20   SS. Fabian and Sebastian's Day

Miles Coverdale, Bishop of
Exeter and Bible translator,
died (1569)

21   St Agnes' Day

First Parliament of King
Henry VIII opened (1510)

22   **St Anastasius' Day**

John Donne, English poet,
was born (1573)

23   William Baffin, English
navigator and explorer, died
(1622)

24   **St Timothy's Day**

Foundation stone of Henry
VII's Lady Chapel at
Westminster Abbey was
laid (1503)

25 Feast of the Conversion of Paul

Probable date of secret
marriage of King Henry
VIII to Anne Boleyn, his
second wife (1533)

26 St Margaret of Scotland's Day

Thomas Howard, 4th Duke
of Norfolk, degraded from
Order of the Garter (1572)

27 St John Chrysostum's Day

Sir Francis Drake, courtier
and explorer, died (1596)

28 **Octave of St Agnes' Day**

King Henry VII of
England was born (1457)

King Henry VIII of
England died (1547)

29 **St Valerius' Day**

Sir Thomas Pope, founder
of Trinity College, Oxford,
died (1559)

30 **St Adelgundis' Day**

Lady Anne Clifford,
Countess of Dorset and
Countess of Pembroke &
Montgomery, was born
(1590)

JANUARY

31 Guy Fawkes was executed
for his role in the
Gunpowder Plot (1606)

Notes

Notes

Month planner

February

1 Queen Elizabeth I signed Mary, Queen of Scots' death warrant (1587)

2 Sir Francis Bryan, 'Vicar of Hell', died (1550)

3 Edward Stafford, 3rd Duke of Buckingham, was born (1478)

4 Anne of York married Lord Thomas Howard (1495)

5 Sir Henry Brooke, diplomat, was born (1537)

6 Shakespeare's *Titus Andronicus* was entered in the Stationers' Register (1594)

7 Thomas Cecil, 1st Earl of Exeter, died (1623)

8 Mary, Queen of Scots was executed at Fotheringhay Castle (1587)

9 Lady Anne Russell, Countess of Warwick, died (1604)

10 Henry, Lord Darnley, husband of Mary, Queen of Scots, was assassinated (1567)

11 Elizabeth of York, Queen Consort of Henry VII and mother of Henry VIII, was born (1466)

12 Lady Jane Grey was executed at the Tower of London (1554)

13 Katheryn Howard, Henry VIII's fifth wife, was executed at the Tower of London (1542)

14 Princess Elizabeth of Great Britain married Frederick V, Elector Palatine (1613)

15 Sir Henry Savile, MP and Provost of Eton, died (1622)

16 Sir William Stanley was executed for treason (1495)

17 Edward Seymour, Earl of Hertford, was created Duke of Somerset (1547)

18 Queen Mary I of England was born (1516)

19 Henry Frederick, Prince of Wales, was born (1594)

20 Edward VI was crowned King of England & Ireland (1547)

21 Ambrose Dudley, 3rd Earl of Warwick, died (1590)

22 Edmund Tudor, Duke of Somerset, was born (1499)

23 Henry Grey, Duke of Suffolk, was executed (1554)

24 Katherine Carey, Countess of Nottingham, died (1603)

25 Robert Devereux, Earl of Essex, was executed for his rebellion against Elizabeth I (1601)

26 Christopher Marlowe, playwright, was baptised (1564)

27 Battle of Ancrum Moor (1545)

28 Stephen Gardiner, Bishop of Winchester and Lord Chancellor, was buried (1556)

29 John Whitgift, Archbishop of Canterbury, died (1604)

Birthdays	Anniversaries	Reminders	Projects

Gardening	Events	Occasions	Festivals

FEBRUARY

1 Queen Elizabeth I signed
Mary, Queen of Scots'
death warrant (1587)

2 **Feast of the Purification of
the Virgin (Candlemas)**

Sir Francis Bryan, 'Vicar of
Hell', died (1550)

3 **St Wereburghe's Day**

Edward Stafford, 3rd Duke
of Buckingham, was born
(1478)

4 **St Gilbert's Day**

Anne of York married Lord
Thomas Howard (1495)

5 **St Abraham of Arbela's
Day**

Sir Henry Brooke,
diplomat, was born (1537)

6 **St Dorothy's Day**

Shakespeare's *Titus
Andronicus* was entered in
the Stationers' Register
(1594)

FEBRUARY

7   Thomas Cecil, 1st Earl
of Exeter, died (1623)

8   Mary, Queen of Scots was
executed at Fotheringhay
Castle (1587)

9   **St Apollonia's Day**

Lady Anne Russell,
Countess of Warwick,
died (1604)

10 Henry, Lord Darnley,
husband of Mary, Queen
of Scots, was assassinated
(1567)

11 Elizabeth of York, Queen
Consort of Henry VII and
mother of Henry VIII,
was born (1466)

12 Lady Jane Grey was
executed at the Tower
of London (1554)

February

13 Katheryn Howard, Henry VIII's fifth wife, was executed at the Tower of London (1542)

14 St Valentine's Day

Princess Elizabeth of Great Britain married Frederick V, Elector Palatine (1613)

15 SS Faustinus and Jovita's Day

Sir Henry Savile, MP and Provost of Eton, died (1622)

16 **St Juliana's Day**

Sir William Stanley was
executed for treason (1495)

17 **Feast of the Flight into Egypt**

Edward Seymour, Earl
of Hertford, was created
Duke of Somerset (1547)

18 **St Simon of Jerusalem's Day**

Queen Mary I of England
was born (1516)

FEBRUARY

19 Henry Frederick, Prince of
Wales, was born (1594)

20 Edward VI was crowned
King of England & Ireland
(1547)

21 Ambrose Dudley, 3rd Earl
of Warwick, died (1590)

22 Edmund Tudor, Duke of
Somerset, was born (1499)

---

23 **St Oswald's Day**

Henry Grey, Duke of
Suffolk, was executed
(1554)

---

24 **St Ethelbert the King's Day**

Katherine Carey, Countess
of Nottingham, died (1603)

FEBRUARY

25 Robert Devereux, Earl of
Essex, was executed for his
rebellion against Elizabeth
I (1601)

26 Christopher Marlowe,
playwright, was baptised
(1564)

27 **St Leander's Day**

Battle of Ancrum Moor
(1545)

28 SS Romanus and Lupicinus' Day

Stephen Gardiner, Bishop
of Winchester and Lord
Chancellor, was buried
(1556)

29 St Matthias' Day

John Whitgift, Archbishop
of Canterbury, died (1604)

Notes

Month Planner

March

1 Corpus Christi College, Oxford was founded (1517)

2 Sir Thomas Bodley, scholar and diplomat, was born (1545)

3 Arthur Plantagenet, 1st Viscount Lisle, died (1542)

4 Sir Henry Carey, 1st Baron Hunsdon, was born (1526)

5 William Oughtred, mathematician, was baptised (1575)

6 Mary I, Queen of England, was married by proxy to Philip II, King of Spain (1554)

7 Sir John Burgh died in a duel (1594)

8 Sir Thomas Tresham, politician, died (1559)

9 David Riccio, private secretary to Mary, Queen of Scots, was assassinated (1566)

10 Thomas Howard, 4th Duke of Norfolk, was born (1536)

11 Lord Henry Brandon, son of Mary, Dowager Queen of France and Duchess of Suffolk, was born (1516)

12 Sir Thomas Boleyn, Earl of Wiltshire and Ormonde, died (1539)

13 Richard Burbage, actor, died (1619)

14 Arthur Bulkeley, Bishop of Bangor, died (1553)

15 John Bull, composer and musician, was buried (1628)

16 Anne Neville, Queen of England, died (1485)

17 King James IV of Scotland was born (1473)

18 Mary, Queen of France and Duchess of Suffolk, was born (1496)

19 Elizabeth Seymour, Countess of Winchester, died (1568)

20 Cicely of York, Viscountess Welles, was born (1469)

21 Pocahontas, daughter of Native American chief Powhatan, was buried at Gravesend, Kent (1617)

22 Katherine Willoughby, 12th Baroness Willoughby d'Eresby, was born (1519)

23 Waltham Abbey surrendered to Henry VIII (1540)

24 Queen Elizabeth I of England died (1603)

25 Sir Walter Raleigh, explorer, granted Letters Patent to discover new territories (1584)

26 Sir Thomas Elyot MP, humanist scholar and diplomat, died (1546)

27 King James VI of Scotland & I of England died (1625)

28 Richard Sackville, 3rd Earl of Dorset, died (1624)

29 Lady Mary Dudley married Sir Henry Sidney (1551)

30 Sir Ralph Sadler, Privy Councillor and diplomat, died (1587)

31 Elizabeth Cavendish, Countess of Lennox, was born (1555)

Birthdays	Anniversaries	Reminders	Projects

Gardening	Events	Occasions	Festivals

MARCH

1 **St David's Day**

Corpus Christi College,
Oxford was founded (1517)

2 **St Cedd's Day (England)**

Sir Thomas Bodley, scholar
and diplomat, was born
(1545)

3 **St Cunigundus' Day**

Arthur Plantagenet, 1st
Viscount Lisle, died (1542)

4   Sir Henry Carey, 1st Baron
Hunsdon, was born (1526)

5   William Oughtred,
mathematician, was
baptised (1575)

6   **St Fridolin's Day**

Mary I, Queen of England,
was married by proxy to
Philip II, King of Spain
(1554)

MARCH

7 **St Thomas Aquinas' Day**

Sir John Burgh died in a
duel (1594)

8 **St Felix' Day**

Sir Thomas Tresham,
politician, died (1559)

9 **Feast of the Forty Martyrs**

David Riccio, private
secretary to Mary, Queen
of Scots, was assassinated
(1566)

10 **St Kessog's Day (Scotland)**

Thomas Howard, 4th Duke
of Norfolk, was born (1536)

11 **St Oswin's Day**

Lord Henry Brandon, son
of Mary, Dowager Queen
of France and Duchess of
Suffolk, was born (1516)

12 **St Gregory the Great's
Day**

Sir Thomas Boleyn, Earl
of Wiltshire and Ormonde,
died (1539)

MARCH

13 **St Kenocha's Day (Scotland)**

Richard Burbage, actor, died (1619)

14 **St Matilda of Ringelheim's Day**

Arthur Bulkeley, Bishop of Bangor, died (1553)

15 **St Longinus' Day**

John Bull, composer and musician, was buried (1628)

16 **St Boniface's Day (Scotland)**

Anne Neville, Queen of England, died (1485)

17 **St Patrick's Day**

King James IV of Scotland was born (1473)

18 **St Cyril's Day**

Mary, Queen of France and Duchess of Suffolk, was born (1496)

MARCH

19 **St Joseph's Day**

Elizabeth Seymour,
Countess of Winchester,
died (1568)

20 **St Cuthbert's Day**

Cicely of York, Viscountess
Welles, was born (1469)

21 **St Benedict of Monte
Cassino's Day**

Pocahontas, daughter of
Native American chief
Powhatan, was buried at
Gravesend, Kent (1617)

22 **St Basil of Ancyra's Day**

Katherine Willoughby,
12th Baroness Willoughby
d'Ereseby, was born (1519)

Easter Sunday – 1573, 1598

23 Waltham Abbey
surrendered to Henry VIII
(1540)

Easter Sunday – 1505, 1516

24 **St Botolph's Day**

Queen Elizabeth I of
England died (1603)

MARCH

25 **Feast of the Annunciation**

Sir Walter Raleigh, explorer, granted Letters Patent to discover new territories (1584)

Easter Sunday – 1543, 1554

26 Sir Thomas Elyot MP, humanist scholar and diplomat, died (1546)

Easter Sunday – 1486, 1497, 1559, 1570, 1581, 1595, 1606, 1617

27 King James VI of Scotland & I of England died (1625)

Easter Sunday – 1502, 1513, 1524, 1622

28 Richard Sackville, 3rd Earl
of Dorset, died (1624)

Easter Sunday – 1529,
1535, 1540

29 Lady Mary Dudley married
Sir Henry Sidney (1551)

Easter Sunday – 1551,
1562, 1587, 1592

30 Sir Ralph Sadler, Privy
Councillor and diplomat,
died (1587)

Easter Sunday – 1494,
1567, 1578, 1603, 1614,
1625

MARCH

31 Elizabeth Cavendish,
Countess of Lennox, was
born (1555)

Easter Sunday – 1499, 1510,
1521, 1532, 1619

Notes

Notes

MONTH PLANNER

April

1   William Harvey, physician, was born (1578)

2   Arthur, Prince of Wales, died (1502)

3   George Herbert, Welsh-born poet, was born (1593)

4   Elizabeth Tilney, Countess of Surrey, died (1497)

5   Thomas Hobbes, philosopher and author, was born (1588)

6   Sir Francis Walsingham, spymaster for Elizabeth I, died (1590)

7   Lady Elizabeth Howard, Countess of Wiltshire, was buried (1538)

8   Dr John Dee made the last entry in his diary (1601)

9   Sir Francis Bacon, philosopher and scientist, died (1626)

10 King James V of Scotland was born (1512)

11 Thomas Wyatt the Younger was executed (1554)

12 Sir William Cecil was made a Knight of the Garter (1553)

13 Guy Fawkes, gunpowder plotter, was born (1570)

14 James Hepburn, Earl of Bothwell, died (1578)

15 Elizabeth Throckmorton, Lady Raleigh, was born (1565)

16 Anne Stanhope, Duchess of Somerset, died (1587)

17 Sir Thomas More was sent to the Tower of London (1534)

18 John Leland, antiquarian, died (1552)

19 Thomas Bastard, clergyman and epigrammatist, died (1618)

20 Lady Mary Grey, cousin of Elizabeth I, died (1578)

21 King Henry VII of England died (1509)

22 Queen Isabella of Castile was born (1451)

23 William Shakespeare, actor, poet and playwright, died (1616)

24 Mary, Queen of Scots married François, Dauphin of France (1558)

25 Sir Edward Howard, Lord High Admiral, died (1513)

26 Katherine Carey married Sir Francis Knollys (1540)

27 David Lewis, first Principal of Jesus College, Oxford, died (1584)

28 Funeral of Queen Elizabeth I of England was held (1603)

29 Thomas Cooper, English Bishop and lexicographer, died (1594)

30 Sir Gilbert Tailboys, husband of Bessie Blount, died (1530)

Birthdays	Anniversaries	Reminders	Projects

Gardening	Events	Occasions	Festivals

APRIL

1 William Harvey, physician, was born (1578)

Easter Sunday – 1526, 1537, 1548, 1584

2 Arthur, Prince of Wales, died (1502)

Easter Sunday – 1460, 1553, 1564, 1589, 1600

3 **St Richard of Chichester's Day**

George Herbert, Welsh-born poet, was born (1593)

Easter Sunday – 1485, 1491, 1496, 1575, 1580, 1611, 1616

4 **St Ambrose's Day**

Elizabeth Tilney, Countess
of Surrey, died (1497)

Easter Sunday – 1507, 1518

5 Thomas Hobbes,
philosopher and author, was
born (1588)

Easter Sunday – 1523,
1534, 1545, 1556

6 **St Celestine's Day**

Sir Francis Walsingham,
spymaster for Elizabeth I,
died (1590)

Easter Sunday – 1488,
1539, 1550, 1561, 1572,
1586, 1597, 1608

APRIL

7 Lady Elizabeth Howard,
Countess of Wiltshire, was
buried (1538)

Easter Sunday – 1493, 1504,
1577, 1602, 1613, 1624

8 Dr John Dee made the last
entry in his diary (1601)

Easter Sunday – 1509, 1515,
1520

9 Sir Francis Bacon,
philosopher and scientist,
died (1626)

Easter Sunday – 1531, 1542

10 King James V of Scotland
was born (1512)

Easter Sunday – 1547,
1558, 1569, 1583, 1594,
1605

11 **St Leo the Great's Day**

Thomas Wyatt the Younger
was executed (1554)

Easter Sunday – 1490,
1501, 1512, 1563, 1574,
1599, 1610, 1621

12 Sir William Cecil was
made a Knight of the
Garter (1553)

Easter Sunday – 1506,
1517, 1528

APRIL

13 St Hermengild's Day (England)

Guy Fawkes, gunpowder plotter, was born (1570)

Easter Sunday – 1533, 1544

14 SS Tibertius, Valerian & Maximus' Day

James Hepburn, Earl of Bothwell, died (1578)

Easter Sunday – 1555, 1560, 1566, 1591, 1596

15 St Magnus of Orkney's Day

Elizabeth Throckmorton, Lady Raleigh, was born (1565)

Easter Sunday – 1487, 1498, 1571, 1582, 1607, 1618

16 Anne Stanhope, Duchess of
Somerset, died (1587)

Easter Sunday – 1503,
1514, 1525, 1536, 1623

17 **St Donanus' Day
(Scotland)**

Sir Thomas More was sent
to the Tower of London
(1534)

Easter Sunday – 1530,
1541, 1552, 1588

18 John Leland, antiquarian,
died (1552)

Easter Sunday – 1557,
1568, 1593, 1604

APRIL

19 **St Leo IX's Day**

Thomas Bastard, clergyman
and epigrammatist, died
(1618)

Easter Sunday – 1489, 1495,
1500, 1579, 1609, 1615,
1620

20 Lady Mary Grey, cousin
of Queen Elizabeth I, died
(1578)

Easter Sunday – 1511, 1522

21 **St Anselm of Canterbury's
Day**

King Henry VII of England
died (1509)

Easter Sunday – 1527, 1538,
1549, 1585

22 Queen Isabella of Castile
was born (1451)

Easter Sunday – 1492,
1565, 1576, 1590, 1601,
1612

23 **St George's Day**

William Shakespeare,
actor, poet and playwright,
died (1616)

Easter Sunday – 1508

24 **St Wilfrid of York's Day**

Mary, Queen of Scots
married François, Dauphin
of France (1558)

Easter Sunday – 1519

APRIL

25 **St Mark the Evangelist's Day**

Sir Edward Howard, Lord High Admiral, died (1513)

Easter Sunday – 1546

26 **SS Cletus and Marcellinus' Day**

Katherine Carey married Sir Francis Knollys (1540)

27 **St Anastasius' Day**

David Lewis, first Principal of Jesus College, Oxford, died (1584)

28 **St Vitalus' Day**

Funeral of Queen Elizabeth
I of England was held
(1603)

29 Thomas Cooper, English
Bishop and lexicographer,
died (1594)

30 **St Catherine of Siena's
Day**

Sir Gilbert Tailboys,
husband of Bessie Blount,
died (1530)

MONTH PLANNER

May

1　Sir William Cavendish was born (1508)

2　Anne Boleyn, Queen of England, was arrested for treason (1536)

3　Margaret of York, Duchess of Burgundy, was born (1446)

4　Edmund de la Pole, Earl of Suffolk, the 'White Rose', was executed (1513)

5　Thomas Cecil, 1st Earl of Exeter, was born (1542)

6　Juan Luis Vives, scholar and tutor to Mary I, died (1540)

7　King James VI of Scotland arrived in London to claim the English throne (1603)

8　Charles Wriothesley, herald and chronicler, was born (1508)

9　John Rouse was elected to office of Bodley's Librarian (1620)

10　Sir Francis Bacon married Alice Barnham (1606)

11　King Henry VII interred in his new chapel at Westminster Abbey (1509)

12　Cardinal Wolsey supervised mass burning of Lutheran books (1521)

13　Battle of Langside (1568)

14　Lady Jean Gordon, Countess of Sutherland, died (1629)

15　Sir Thomas Bromley, judge, died (1555)

16　Patrick Ruthven, 3rd Lord Ruthven, died (1566)

17　Anne of Denmark, wife of James VI, was crowned Queen of Scotland (1590)

18　Katherine Woodville, Duchess of Buckingham, died (1497)

19　Anne Boleyn, Henry VIII's second wife, was executed (1536)

20　King Henry VIII and Jane Seymour were betrothed (1536)

21　Philip, King of Spain and King Consort of England, was born (1527)

22　Edward Seymour, Viscount Beauchamp and Earl of Hertford, was born (probably) (1539)

23　Elias Ashmole, founder of the Ashmolean Museum, was born (1617)

24　Elizabeth Carey, Lady Berkeley, was born (1576)

25　Lady Jane Grey married Lord Guilford Dudley (1553)

26　Sir Anthony Fitzherbert, judge and legal writer, died (1538)

27　Lady Margaret Pole, Countess of Salisbury, was executed (1541)

28　First ships of the Spanish Armada left Lisbon (1588)

29　Cardinal David Beaton assassinated at St Andrews (1546)

30　King Henry VIII of England married his third wife, Jane Seymour (1536)

31　Lady Margaret Beaufort, Countess of Richmond & Derby, mother of Henry VII, was born (1443)

Birthdays	Anniversaries	Reminders	Projects

Gardening	Events	Occasions	Festivals

MAY

1 **SS Philip and James the Less, the Apostles' Day**

Sir William Cavendish was born (1508)

2 Anne Boleyn, Queen of England, was arrested for treason (1536)

3 **SS Alexander, Eventius and Theolous' Day**

Margaret of York, Duchess of Burgundy, was born (1446)

4   **St Anthony of Tours' Day**

Edmund de la Pole, Earl of
Suffolk, the 'White Rose',
was executed (1513)

5   Thomas Cecil, 1st Earl of
Exeter, was born (1542)

6   **St John the Evangelist's
Day**

Juan Luis Vives, scholar
and tutor to Mary I, died
(1540)

MAY

7 King James VI of Scotland
arrived in London to claim
the English throne (1603)

8 **Feast of the Archangel
Michael**

Charles Wriothesley, herald
and chronicler, was born
(1508)

9 **St Nicholas of Myra's Day**

John Rouse was elected to
office of Bodley's Librarian
(1620)

10 St Aurelian of Limoge's Day

Sir Francis Bacon married
Alice Barnham (1606)

11 St Mamertus' Day

King Henry VII interred
in his new chapel at
Westminster Abbey (1509)

12 SS Nereus and Achilleus' Day

Cardinal Wolsey supervised
mass burning of Lutheran
books (1521)

MAY

13   Battle of Langside (1568)

14   **St Boniface's Day**

Lady Jean Gordon,
Countess of Sutherland,
died (1629)

15   Sir Thomas Bromley, judge,
died (1555)

16 Patrick Ruthven, 3rd Lord
Ruthven, died (1566)

17 Anne of Denmark, wife
of James VI, was crowned
Queen of Scotland (1590)

18 Katherine Woodville,
Duchess of Buckingham,
died (1497)

MAY

19 **St Pudentiana's Day**

Anne Boleyn, Henry VIII's
second wife, was executed
(1536)

20 King Henry VIII and Jane
Seymour were betrothed
(1536)

21 Philip, King of Spain and
King Consort of England,
was born (1527)

22 Edward Seymour, Viscount
Beauchamp and Earl
of Hertford, was born
(probably) (1539)

23 Elias Ashmole, founder of
the Ashmolean Museum,
was born (1617)

24 Elizabeth Carey, Lady
Berkeley, was born (1576)

MAY

25 **SS Gregory VII and Urban's Day**

Lady Jane Grey married
Lord Guilford Dudley
(1553)

26 **St Augustine of Canterbury's Day**

Sir Anthony Fitzherbert,
judge and legal writer, died
(1538)

27 Lady Margaret Pole,
Countess of Salisbury,
was executed (1541)

28 **St Bridget of Sweden's Day**

First ships of the Spanish
Armada left Lisbon (1588)

29 Cardinal David Beaton
assassinated at St Andrews
(1546)

30 King Henry VIII of
England married his third
wife, Jane Seymour (1536)

MAY

31 **Feast of The Visitation**

Lady Margaret Beaufort,
Countess of Richmond &
Derby, mother of Henry
VII, was born (1443)

Cicely Neville, Duchess of
York, mother of Edward IV
and Richard III, died (1495)

Notes

Notes

MONTH PLANNER

June

1 Anne Boleyn was crowned Queen of England (1533)

2 James Douglas, 4th Earl of Morton, formerly Regent of Scotland, was executed (1581)

3 Earl of Essex' expedition leaves for Cadiz, Spain (1596)

4 Major fire devastated St Paul's, London, after a lightning strike (1561)

5 *Tottel's Miscellany*, the first anthology of English verse, was published (1557)

6 William Hunnis, musician and conspirator, died (1597)

7 King Henry VIII and King François I met at the Field of Cloth of Gold (1520)

8 Elizabeth Woodville, Dowager Queen of England, died (1492)

9 Use of 1549 Book of Common Prayer became mandatory in all churches in England and Wales (1549)

10 François, Duke of Anjou, died (1584)

11 Marie of Guise, Queen-regent of Scotland, died (1560)

12 Sir Richard Rich, 1st Baron Rich, died (1567)

13 *Henry Grâce à Dieu* ('Great Harry') was consecrated (1514)

14 Thomas Wharton, 2nd Baron Wharton, died (1572)

15 Battle of Carberry Hill (1567)

16 Battle of Stoke (1487)

17 King James V of Scotland married his second wife, Marie of Guise (1538)

18 Mary, Queen of Scots was imprisoned at Lochleven Castle (1567)

19 King James VI of Scotland and I of England was born (1566)

20 Lady Margaret Douglas, Countess of Lennox, was sent to the Tower of London (1565)

21 John Skelton, poet, satirist and one of Henry VIII's tutors, died (1529)

22 Sir William Carey, courtier and husband of Mary Boleyn, died (1528)

23 Levina Teerlinc, miniaturist, died (1576)

24 Henry VIII and Katharine of Aragon were crowned King and Queen of England (1509)

25 Mary Tudor, Dowager Queen of France and Duchess of Suffolk, died (1533)

26 Richard III was crowned King of England (1483)

27 Jesus College, Oxford, received its royal charter (1571)

28 King Henry VIII of England was born (1491)

29 Lady Margaret Beaufort, Countess of Richmond & Derby and mother of Henry VII, died (1509)

30 Thomas, Lord Darcy of Temple Hurst, was executed (1537)

Birthdays	Anniversaries	Reminders	Projects

Gardening	Events	Occasions	Festivals

JUNE

1 **St Justin's Day**

Anne Boleyn was crowned
Queen of England (1533)

2 **SS Marcellinus and Peter's
Day**

James Douglas, 4th Earl of
Morton, formerly Regent
of Scotland, was executed
(1581)

3 Earl of Essex' expedition
leaves for Cadiz, Spain
(1596)

4 **St Petroc's Day**

Major fire devastated St
Paul's, London, after a
lightning strike (1561)

5 **SS Boniface and
companions' Day**

Tottel's Miscellany, the first
anthology of English verse,
was published (1557)

6 William Hunnis, musician
and conspirator, died (1597)

JUNE

7 **St Paul of Constantinople's Day**

King Henry VIII and King François I met at the Field of Cloth of Gold (1520)

8 Elizabeth Woodville, Dowager Queen of England, died (1492)

9 **SS Primus and Felicianus' Days**

The use of the 1549 Book of Common Prayer became mandatory in all churches in England and Wales (1549)

10 François, Duke of Anjou, died (1584)

11 **SS Basilides and Companions Day**

King Henry VIII of England married his first wife, Katharine of Aragon (1509)

Marie of Guise, Queen-regent of Scotland, died (1560)

12 Sir Richard Rich, 1st Baron Rich, died (1567)

JUNE

13 **St Anthony of Padua's Day**

Henry Grâce à Dieu ('Great Harry') was consecrated (1514)

14 Thomas Wharton, 2nd Baron Wharton, died (1572)

15 Battle of Carberry Hill (1567)

16 **St Margaret of Scotland's Day**

Battle of Stoke (1487)

17 King James V of Scotland married his second wife, Marie of Guise (1538)

18 **SS Marcus and Marcellianus' Day**

Mary, Queen of Scots was imprisoned at Lochleven Castle (1567)

JUNE

19 **SS Gervasius and Protasius Day**

King James VI of Scotland and I of England was born (1566)

20 **St Edward, King and Martyr's Day**

Lady Margaret Douglas, Countess of Lennox, was sent to the Tower of London (1565)

21 John Skelton, poet, satirist and one of Henry VIII's tutors, died (1529)

22 **St Alban's Day**

Sir William Carey, courtier
and husband of Mary
Boleyn, died (1528)

23 **St Etheldreda's Day**

Levina Teerlinc,
miniaturist, died (1576)

24 **St John the Baptist's Day**

Henry VIII and Katharine
of Aragon were crowned
King and Queen of
England (1509)

JUNE

25 Mary Tudor, Dowager
Queen of France and
Duchess of Suffolk, died
(1533)

_____

_____

_____

_____

_____

_____

_____

_____

26 Richard III was crowned
King of England (1483)

_____

_____

_____

_____

_____

_____

_____

_____

27 **St Cyril of Alexandria's
Day**

Jesus College, Oxford,
received its royal charter
(1571)

_____

_____

_____

_____

_____

_____

_____

_____

28 **St Irenaeus' Day**

King Henry VIII of
England was born (1491)

29 **Feast of SS Peter and Paul,
the Apostles**

Lady Margaret Beaufort,
Countess of Richmond
& Derby and mother of
Henry VII, died (1509)

30 Thomas, Lord Darcy
of Temple Hurst, was
executed (1537)

Month Planner

July

1 Treaties of Greenwich, between Scotland and England, were signed (1543)

2 Thomas Cranmer, Archbishop of Canterbury, was born (1489)

3 Sir Edward Fitton, administrator and Vice-Treasurer for Elizabeth I, died (1579)

4 William Byrd, Elizabethan composer, died (1623)

5 Gregory Cromwell, 1st Baron Cromwell, died (1551)

6 King Edward VI of England died (1553)

7 Lady Penelope Devereux, Lady Rich, died (1607)

8 Mary, daughter of Henry VIII, proclaimed herself queen (1553)

9 Marriage of King Henry VIII and Anne of Cleves was annulled (1540)

10 Lady Jane Grey was proclaimed queen in London by the Privy Council (1553)

11 Pope drew up Bull of Excommunication against Henry VIII and Thomas Cranmer (1533)

12 King Henry VIII married his sixth wife, Katherine Parr (1543)

13 Dr John Dee, astrologer and adviser to Elizabeth I, was born (1527)

14 The brothers, Lord Henry and Lord Charles Brandon, died (1551)

15 Inigo Jones, architect and theatre designer, was born (1573)

16 Anne of Cleves, fourth wife of Henry VIII, died (1557)

17 Janet Douglas, Lady Glamis, was burnt for treason (1537)

18 King Henry VII entered the Holy League or League of Venice (1496)

19 *Mary Rose*, one of the largest ships in King Henry VIII's navy, sank in the Solent (1545)

20 Anne Knollys, Baroness de la Warr, was born (1555)

21 Hostile French forces landed at the Isle of Wight (1545)

22 John Scrope, 5th Baron Scrope of Bolton, was born (c.1437)

23 Henry Carey, 1st Baron Hunsdon, died (1596)

24 Mary, Queen of Scots was forced to abdicate (1567)

25 King James VI of Scotland was crowned King James I of England (1603)

26 George Talbot, 4th Earl of Shrewsbury & 4th Earl of Waterford, died (1538)

27 Lady Jane FitzAlan (Lady Lumley), translator, died (1578)

28 Thomas Cromwell, Earl of Essex, was executed (1540)

29 Mary, Queen of Scots, married Henry Stuart, Lord Darnley (1565)

30 Anne Woodville, Viscountess Bourchier, died (1489)

31 Edmund Sheffield, 1st Baron Sheffield, died (1549)

Birthdays	Anniversaries	Reminders	Projects

Gardening	Events	Occasions	Festivals

JULY

1 **Octave of Feast of St John the Baptist**

Treaties of Greenwich, between Scotland and England, were signed (1543)

2 **The Feast of the Visitation**

Thomas Cranmer, Archbishop of Canterbury, was born (1489)

3 Sir Edward Fitton, administrator and Vice-Treasurer for Elizabeth I, died (1579)

4 **St Ulrig of Augsburg's Day**

William Byrd, Elizabethan composer, died (1623)

5 Gregory Cromwell, 1st Baron Cromwell, died (1551)

6 **Octave of Feast of SS Peter and Paul**

King Edward VI of England died (1553)

July

7 Lady Penelope Devereux, Lady Rich, died (1607)

8 **St Elizabeth of Portugal's Day**

Mary, daughter of Henry VIII, proclaimed herself queen (1553)

9 **Octave of the Visitation**

Marriage of King Henry VIII and Anne of Cleves was annulled (1540)

10 **SS Rufina and Secunda's Day**

Lady Jane Grey was proclaimed queen in London by the Privy Council (1553)

11 **St Benedict's Day**

Pope drew up Bull of Excommunication against Henry VIII and Thomas Cranmer (1533)

12 **SS Nabor and Felix's Day**

King Henry VIII married his sixth wife, Katherine Parr (1543)

JULY

13 Dr John Dee, astrologer
and adviser to Elizabeth I,
was born (1527)

14 The brothers, Lord Henry
and Lord Charles Brandon,
died (1551)

15 **St Swithun's Day**

Inigo Jones, architect and
theatre designer, was born
(1573)

16 Anne of Cleves, fourth wife of Henry VIII, died (1557)

17 **St Alexius's Day**

Janet Douglas, Lady Glamis, was burnt for treason (1537)

18 **St Edburga's Day**

King Henry VII entered the Holy League or League of Venice (1496)

19 **St Arsenius' Day**

Mary Rose, one of the
largest ships in Henry VIII's
navy, and the flagship of
Admiral Carew, sank in the
Solent (1545)

20 **St Margaret of Antioch's
Day**

Anne Knollys, Baroness de
la Warr, was born (1555)

21 Hostile French forces
landed at the Isle of Wight
(1545)

22 St Mary Magdalene's Day

John Scrope, 5th Baron
Scrope of Bolton, was born
(c.1437)

23 St Apollinarus' Day

Henry Carey, 1st Baron
Hunsdon, died (1596)

24 St Christina's Day

Mary, Queen of Scots was
forced to abdicate (1567)

JULY

25 **Feast of the Apostle James the Great**

King James VI of Scotland was crowned King James I of England (1603)

26 **St Anne's Day**

George Talbot, 4th Earl of Shrewsbury & 4th Earl of Waterford, died (1538)

27 Lady Jane FitzAlan (Lady Lumley), translator, died (1578)

28 **St Panatleon's Day**

Thomas Cromwell, Earl of
Essex, was executed (1540)

King Henry VIII married
Katheryn Howard, his fifth
wife (1540)

29 **St Martha's Day**

Mary, Queen of Scots,
married Henry Stuart,
Lord Darnley (1565)

Baby son of Mary Queen
of Scots was crowned
King James VI (1567)

30 **SS Abdon and Sennen's
Day**

Anne Woodville,
Viscountess Bourchier,
died (1489)

July

31 St Fabius' Day

Edmund Sheffield, 1st
Baron Sheffield, died (1549)

Notes

Notes

Month Planner

August

1 Sir Edward Kelley, apothecary and alchemist, was born (1555)

2 Vice Admiral Sir Richard Leveson died (1605)

3 Sir Robert Houghton, Treasurer & Sergeant-at-Law, was born (1548)

4 William Cecil, Lord Burghley, died (1598)

5 Sir Reginald Bray, Henry VII's chief tax adviser, died (1503)

6 Margaret, Dowager Queen of Scots, married Archibald Douglas, 6th Earl of Angus (1514)

7 Sir Robert Dudley, mariner and cartographer, was born (1574)

8 Princess Margaret of England married King James IV of Scots (1503)

9 John Blagrave, mathematician and land surveyor, died (1611)

10 Madeleine of Valois, Queen of Scots, was born (1520)

11 Joan Beaufort, Lady Howth, died (1518)

12 Ursula Pole, Lady Stafford, died (1570)

13 Sir Humphrey Radcliffe, MP, died (1566)

14 Lady Margaret Pole, Countess of Salisbury, was born (1473)

15 Mary Shelton, Lady Scudamore, was buried (1603)

16 Battle of the Spurs (1513)

17 John Scrope, 5th Baron Scrope of Bolton, died (1498)

18 William Borough, Comptroller of the Queen's Ships, was baptised (1536)

19 Princess Elizabeth of Great Britain, Queen of Bohemia, was born (1596)

20 Sir William Cavendish and Elizabeth Hardwick were married (1547)

21 Humphrey Llwyd, translater and cartographer, died (1568)

22 King Richard III was killed at the Battle of Bosworth Field (1485)

23 Stephen Gardiner, Bishop of Winchester, was appointed Lord Chancellor (1553)

24 Cicely of York, Viscountess Welles, died (1507)

25 Lady Katherine Grey, Countess of Hertford, was born (1540)

26 Sir Clement Smith, administrator, died (1552)

27 Katharine of Aragon, Regent of England, issued warrants for confiscation of all lands held by Scots in England (1513)

28 Sir Francis Drake and Sir John Hawkins departed England on their final voyage (1595)

29 Sir Thomas Offley, Mayor of London, died (1582)

30 Mary Seymour, daughter of Dowager Queen Katherine Parr, was born (1548)

31 William Llyn, foremost Welsh bard, died (1580)

Birthdays	Anniversaries	Reminders	Projects

Gardening	Events	Occasions	Festivals

AUGUST

1   **Feast of the Maccabees**

Sir Edward Kelley,
apothecary and alchemist,
was born (1555)

2   **Pope St Stephen I's Day**

Vice Admiral Sir Richard
Leveson died (1605)

3   **St Walthen of Melrose's
Day**

Sir Robert Houghton,
Treasurer & Sergeant-at-
Law, was born (1548)

4 William Cecil, Lord
Burghley, died (1598)

5 Sir Reginald Bray, Henry
VII's chief tax adviser, died
(1503)

6 **Feast of the
Transfiguration**

Margaret, Dowager Queen
of Scots, married Archibald
Douglas, 6th Earl of Angus
(1514)

AUGUST

7 **St Sixtus II and Companions' Day**

Sir Robert Dudley, mariner and cartographer, was born (1574)

8 **St Cyriacus and Companions' Day**

Princess Margaret of England married King James IV of Scots (1503)

9 John Blagrave, mathematician and land surveyor, died (1611)

10 **St Lawrence's Day**

Madeleine of Valois, Queen of Scots, was born (1520)

11 Joan Beaufort, Lady Howth, died (1518)

12 **St Clare's Day**

Ursula Pole, Lady Stafford, died (1570)

AUGUST

13 Sir Humphrey Radcliffe, MP, died (1566)

14 **Vigil of the Assumption of the Blessed Virgin**

Lady Margaret Pole, Countess of Salisbury, was born (1473)

15 **Assumption of the Blessed Virgin**

Mary Shelton, Lady Scudamore, was buried (1603)

16   Battle of the Spurs (1513)

17   **Octave of St Lawrence's Day**

John Scrope, 5th Baron Scrope of Bolton, died (1498)

18   **St Helena's Day**

William Borough, Comptroller of the Queen's Ships, was baptised (1536)

AUGUST

19 Princess Elizabeth of Great
Britain, Queen of Bohemia,
was born (1596)

20 **St Bernard's Day**

Sir William Cavendish and
Elizabeth Hardwick were
married (1547)

21 Humphrey Llwyd,
translater and cartographer,
died (1568)

22 **Octave of the Assumption**

Battle of Bosworth Field (1485)

King Richard III was killed at the Battle of Bosworth Field (1485)

23 Stephen Gardiner, Bishop of Winchester, was appointed Lord Chancellor (1553)

24 **St Bartholomew the Apostle's Day**

Cicely of York, Viscountess Welles, died (1507)

AUGUST

25 **St Louis IX's Day**

Lady Katherine Grey,
Countess of Hertford, was
born (1540)

26 Sir Clement Smith,
administrator, died (1552)

27 Katharine of Aragon,
Regent of England, issued
warrants for confiscation
of all lands held by Scots in
England (1513)

28 **St Augustine of Hippo's Day**

Sir Francis Drake and Sir John Hawkins departed England on their final voyage (1595)

29 Sir Thomas Offley, Mayor of London, died (1582)

30 **SS Felix and Adauctus' Day**

Mary Seymour, daughter of Dowager Queen Katherine Parr, was born (1548)

AUGUST

31 William Llyn, foremost
Welsh bard, died (1580)

Notes

Notes

Month Planner

September

1   Anne Boleyn was created Lady Marquis of Pembroke (1532)

2   Sir Richard Grenville, naval commander and explorer, died at sea (1591)

3   Gerald Fitzgerald, 8th Earl of Kildare, died (1513)

4   Robert Dudley, Earl of Leicester, died (1588)

5   Katherine Parr, Dowager Queen of England, died (1548)

6   Sir Richard Guildford, courtier, died in Jerusalem (1506)

7   Elizabeth I, Queen of England, was born (1533)

8   Amy Robsart, Lady Dudley, died (1560)

9   King James IV was killed at the Battle of Flodden (1513)

10   Battle of Pinkie Cleugh (1547)

11   Thomas Kitson the Elder, Sheriff of London, died (1540)

12   François I, King of France, was born (1494)

13   Sir John Cheke, scholar and tutor to Edward VI, died (1557)

14   Sir William Kingston, Constable of the Tower of London, died (1540)

15   John Morton, Archbishop of Canterbury and Chancellor to Henry VII, died (1500)

16   John Colet, scholar and Dean of St Paul's, died (1519)

17   Charles Howard, 2nd Earl of Nottingham, was born (1579)

18   Henry Stafford, 1st Baron Stafford, was born (1501)

19   Katherine Willoughby, 12th Baroness Willoughby d'Eresby, died (1580)

20   Arthur, Prince of Wales, was born (1486)

21   Robert Dudley, Earl of Leicester, married Lettice Knollys (1578)

22   Anne of Cleves, Queen of England, was born (1515)

23   Katherine Pole, Countess of Huntingdon, died (1571)

24   Edward Seymour, Viscount Beauchamp, was born in the Tower of London (1561)

25   Gregory Fiennes, 10th Baron Dacre, died (1594)

26   Francis Drake completed his circumnavigation of the globe (1580)

27   Lady Eleanor Brandon, Countess of Cumberland, died (1547)

28   Francis Talbot, 5th Earl of Shrewsbury, died (1560)

29   Lord Robert Dudley was created Earl of Leicester (1564)

30   Lady Frances Devereux, Duchess of Somerset, was born (1599)

Birthdays	Anniversaries	Reminders	Projects

Gardening	Events	Occasions	Festivals

SEPTEMBER

1   **St Priscus' Day**

Anne Boleyn was created
Lady Marquis of Pembroke
(1532)

2   Sir Richard Grenville, naval
commander and explorer,
died at sea (1591)

3   **St Gregory the Great's Day**

Gerald Fitzgerald, 8th Earl
of Kildare, died (1513)

4 **St Cuthbert's Day**

Robert Dudley, Earl of
Leicester, died (1588)

5 Katherine Parr, Dowager
Queen of England, died
(1548)

6 Sir Richard Guildford,
courtier, died in Jerusalem
(1506)

SEPTEMBER

7   **Vigil of the Nativity of the Blessed Virgin**

Elizabeth I, Queen of England, was born (1533)

8   **Feast of the Nativity of the Blessed Virgin**

Amy Robsart, Lady Dudley, died (1560)

9   Battle of Flodden (1513)

King James IV was killed at the Battle of Flodden (1513)

10 Battle of Pinkie Cleugh
(1547)

11 Thomas Kitson the Elder,
Sheriff of London, died
(1540)

12 François I, King of France,
was born (1494)

SEPTEMBER

13 Sir John Cheke, scholar and
tutor to Edward VI, died
(1557)

14 Sir William Kingston,
Constable of the Tower of
London, died (1540)

15 **Octave of the Nativity of
the Blessed Virgin**

John Morton, Archbishop of
Canterbury and Chancellor
to Henry VII, died (1500)

16 **SS Cornelius and Cyprian's Day**

John Colet, scholar and Dean of St Paul's, died (1519)

17 **St Lambert's Day**

Charles Howard, 2nd Earl of Nottingham, was born (1579)

18 Henry Stafford, 1st Baron Stafford, was born (1501)

SEPTEMBER

19 Katherine Willoughby,
12th Baroness Willoughby
d'Eresby, died (1580)

20 Arthur, Prince of Wales,
was born (1486)

21 **St Matthew the Apostle's
Day**

Robert Dudley, Earl of
Leicester, married Lettice
Knollys (1578)

22 Anne of Cleves, Queen of
England, was born (1515)

23 **St Thecla's Day**

Katherine Pole, Countess of
Huntingdon, died (1571)

24 **Feast of the Conception of
St John the Baptist**

Edward Seymour, Viscount
Beauchamp, was born
in the Tower of London
(1561)

SEPTEMBER

25 Gregory Fiennes, 10th
Baron Dacre, died (1594)

26 **St Cyprian's Day**

Francis Drake completed
his circumnavigation of the
globe (1580)

27 Lady Eleanor Brandon,
Countess of Cumberland,
died (1547)

28 St Wenceslas of Bohemia's Day

Francis Talbot, 5th Earl of Shrewsbury, died (1560)

29 Feast of St Michael and All Angels (Michaelmas)

Lord Robert Dudley was created Earl of Leicester (1564)

30 St Jerome's Day

Lady Frances Devereux, Duchess of Somerset, was born (1599)

MONTH PLANNER

October

1   Mary I was crowned Queen of England (1553)

2   Richard III, King of England, was born (1452)

3   Sir William Fitzwilliam, Gentleman of Edward VI's Privy Chamber, died (1559)

4   Henry Stanley, 4th Earl of Derby, was baptised (1531)

5   Edward Wotton, physician and naturalist, died (1555)

6   John Caius, Royal Physician and founder of Gonville and Caius College, Cambridge, was born (1510)

7   Lady Margaret Douglas, Countess of Lennox, was born (1515)

8   Edward Wright, mathematician and cartographer, was baptised (1561)

9   Princess Mary of England married Louis XII of France (1514)

10 Elizabeth I, Queen of England, was taken ill with smallpox (1562)

11 Sir Thomas Wyatt the Elder, poet and diplomat, died (1542)

12 Edward VI, King of England, was born (1537)

13 Sir Edward Waterhouse, administrator, died (1591)

14 Thomas Chaloner, ambassador and poet, died (1565)

15 William Fitzwilliam, 1st Earl of Southampton, died (1542)

16 Thomas Davies, Bishop of St Asaph, died (1573)

17 Sir Philip Sidney, poet, courtier and soldier, died (1586)

18 Margaret Tudor, Dowager Queen of Scots, died (1541)

19 Anthony Browne, 1st Viscount Montagu, died (1592)

20 Mary Arundell, Countess of Sussex and Countess of Arundel, died (1557)

21 John Dudley, 2nd Earl of Warwick, died after he was released from Tower of London (1554)

22 Sir Edward Poynings, soldier, administrator and diplomat, died (1521)

23 Sir John Gresham, Lord Mayor of London, died (1556)

24 Jane Seymour, Queen of England, died (1537)

25 Sir William Cavendish, courtier and Privy Councillor, died (1557)

26 Sir Robert Southwell, lawyer and MP, died (1559)

27 Jasper Tudor, uncle of Henry VII, was created Duke of Bedford (1485)

28 Sir John Gage, Privy Councillor and Constable for the Tower, was born (1479)

29 Sir Walter Raleigh, courtier and explorer, was executed (1618)

30 Henry VII was crowned King of England (1485)

31 Lord Thomas Howard died in the Tower of London (1537)

Birthdays	Anniversaries	Reminders	Projects

Gardening	Events	Occasions	Festivals

OCTOBER

1   Mary I was crowned Queen
     of England (1553)

2   Richard III, King of
     England, was born (1452)

3   Sir William Fitzwilliam,
     Gentleman of Edward VI's
     Privy Chamber, died (1559)

4   **St Francis of Assisi's Day**

Henry Stanley, 4th Earl of
Derby, was baptised (1531)

5   Edward Wotton, physician
and naturalist, died (1555)

6   **St Faith's Day**

John Caius, Royal
Physician and founder
of Gonville and Caius
College, Cambridge, was
born (1510)

OCTOBER

7   **SS Marcellus and Apuleius' Day**

Lady Margaret Douglas, Countess of Lennox, was born (1515)

8   Edward Wright, mathematician and cartographer, was baptised (1561)

9   Princess Mary of England married Louis XII of France (1514)

10 Elizabeth I, Queen of England, was taken ill with smallpox (1562)

11 Sir Thomas Wyatt the Elder, poet and diplomat, died (1542)

12 **St Wilfrid of York's Day**

Edward VI, King of England, was born (1537)

OCTOBER

13 Sir Edward Waterhouse,
administrator, died (1591)

14 Thomas Chaloner,
ambassador and poet, died
(1565)

15 **St Wulfram of Sens' Day**

William Fitzwilliam, 1st
Earl of Southampton, died
(1542)

16 Thomas Davies, Bishop of
St Asaph, died (1573)

17 **St Ignatius' Day**

Sir Philip Sidney, poet,
courtier and soldier, died
(1586)

18 **St Luke the Evangelist's
Day**

Margaret Tudor, Dowager
Queen of Scots, died (1541)

19 Anthony Browne, 1st
Viscount Montagu, died
(1592)

20 Mary Arundell, Countess
of Sussex and Countess of
Arundel, died (1557)

21 **Feast of the Eleven
Thousand Virgins**

John Dudley, 2nd Earl of
Warwick, died after he
was released from Tower of
London (1554)

22 Sir Edward Poynings,
soldier, administrator and
diplomat, died (1521)

23 Sir John Gresham, Lord
Mayor of London, died
(1556)

24 Jane Seymour, Queen of
England, died (1537)

25 SS Crispin and Crispinian's Day

Sir William Cavendish, courtier and Privy Councillor, died (1557)

26 Sir Robert Southwell, lawyer and MP, died (1559)

27 Vigil of Feast of SS Simon and Jude

Jasper Tudor, uncle of Henry VII, was created Duke of Bedford (1485)

Lord Thomas Stanley, step-father to Henry VII, was created Earl of Derby (1485)

28 **Feast of SS Simon and Jude, Apostles**

Sir John Gage, Privy Councillor and Constable for the Tower, was born (1479)

29 Sir Walter Raleigh, courtier and explorer, was executed (1618)

30 Henry VII was crowned King of England (1485)

OCTOBER

31 **All Hallows' Eve**

Lord Thomas Howard died
in the Tower of London
(1537)

Notes

Notes

MONTH PLANNER

November

1   Edmund Tudor, Earl of Richmond, died (1456)

2   Edward V, King of England, was born (1470)

3   Nicholas Carr, physician and scholar, died (1568)

4   Henry Pole, 1st Baron Montagu, was arrested for treason (1538)

5   Guy Fawkes was caught with 36 barrels of gunpowder beneath Westminster (1605)

6   Sir Thomas Roe, diplomat, died (1644)

7   Sir Edward Warner, Lieutenant of the Tower of London, died (1565)

8   The Bodleian Library, Oxford, first opened to the public (1602)

9   Katharine of Aragon, Queen of England, gave birth to a daughter who died at birth (1518)

10 Robert Devereux, 2nd Earl of Essex, was born (1565)

11 Richard Madox, diarist and clergyman, was born (1546)

12 Sir John Hawkins, navigator and explorer, died on a voyage with Sir Francis Drake (1595)

13 Trial of Lady Jane Grey and her husband, Lord Guilford Dudley, took place (1553)

14 Arthur, Prince of Wales, married Katharine of Aragon (1501)

15 Katherine of York, Countess of Devon, died (1527)

16 Charles Neville, 6th Earl of Westmorland, died in Flanders (1601)

17 Mary I, Queen of England, died (1558)

18 Cuthbert Tunstall, Bishop of Durham, died in prison (1559)

19 Charles I, King of England, was born (1600)

20 Marie of Guise, Queen Consort and Regent of Scotland, was born (1515)

21 Lady Frances Brandon, Duchess of Suffolk, died (1559)

22 Sir William Butts, physician, died (1545)

23 Perkin Warbeck, pretender to the throne, was hanged (1499)

24 Battle of Solway Moss (1542)

25 Thomas Dacre, 2nd Baron of Gilsland, was born (1467)

26 Henry Fitzroy, Duke of Richmond and Somerset, married Lady Mary Howard (1533)

27 William Shakespeare married Anne Hathaway (1582)

28 Margaret Tudor, Queen of Scots, was born (1489)

29 Thomas Wolsey, Cardinal and Archbishop of York, died (1529)

30 Sir Philip Sidney, poet and courtier, was born (1554)

Birthdays	Anniversaries	Reminders	Projects

Gardening	Events	Occasions	Festivals

November

1 **All Hallows' Day**

Edmund Tudor, Earl of
Richmond, died (1456)

2 **All Souls' Day**

Edward V, King of
England, was born (1470)

Anne of York was born
(1475)

3 Nicholas Carr, physician
and scholar, died (1568)

4 Henry Pole, 1st Baron
Montagu, was arrested for
treason (1538)

5 Guy Fawkes was caught
with 36 barrels of
gunpowder beneath
Westminster (1605)

6 **St Leonard's Day**

Sir Thomas Roe, diplomat,
died (1644)

November

7   Sir Edward Warner,
Lieutenant of the Tower of
London, died (1565)

---

8   **Feast of the Four Crowned Martyrs**

The Bodleian Library,
Oxford, first opened to the
public (1602)

---

9   Katharine of Aragon,
Queen of England, gave
birth to a daughter
who died at birth (1518)

---

10   Robert Devereux, 2nd Earl
of Essex, was born (1565)

11   **St Martin of Tours' Day
(Martinmas)**

Richard Madox, diarist and
clergyman, was born (1546)

12   **St Macarius' Day**

Sir John Hawkins,
navigator and explorer,
died on a voyage with Sir
Francis Drake (1595)

NOVEMBER

13 **St Brictius' Day**

Trial of Lady Jane Grey and
her husband, Lord Guilford
Dudley, took place (1553)

14 Arthur, Prince of Wales,
married Katharine of
Aragon (1501)

15 Katherine of York, Countess
of Devon, died (1527)

16   **St Margaret of Scotland's Day**

Charles Neville, 6th Earl of Westmorland, died in Flanders (1601)

17   **St Hilda of Whitby's Day**

Mary I, Queen of England, died (1558)

Cardinal Reginald Pole, Archbishop of Canterbury, died (1558)

18   **Octave of Martinmas**

Cuthbert Tunstall, Bishop of Durham, died in prison (1559)

November

19 **St Elizabeth's Day**

Charles I, King of England,
was born (1600)

20 Marie of Guise, Queen
Consort and Regent of
Scotland, was born (1515)

21 **Feast of the Presentation of
the Blessed Virgin**

Lady Frances Brandon,
Duchess of Suffolk, died
(1559)

22 St Cecilia's Day

Sir William Butts,
physician, died (1545)

23 Pope St Clement I's Day

Perkin Warbeck, pretender
to the throne, was hanged
(1499)

24 St Crisogonus' Day

Battle of Solway Moss
(1542)

25 St Catherine of Alexandria's Day

Thomas Dacre, 2nd Baron of Gilsland, was born (1467)

26 St Conrad of Constance's Day

Henry Fitzroy, Duke of Richmond and Somerset, married Lady Mary Howard (1533)

27 SS Vitalis and Agricola's Day

William Shakespeare married Anne Hathaway (1582)

28 Margaret Tudor, Queen of
Scots, was born (1489)

---

29 **Vigil of St Andrew the
Apostle**

Thomas Wolsey, Cardinal
and Archbishop of York,
died (1529)

---

30 **Feast of St Andrew the
Apostle**

Sir Philip Sidney, poet and
courtier, was born (1554)

Month Planner

December

1 Maud Green, Lady Parr, died (1531)

2 Henry Howard, Earl of Surrey, was arrested and sent to the Tower of London (1546)

3 Sir Charles Brandon was given wardship and marriage of Elizabeth, Viscountess Lisle (1511)

4 William Whitaker, theologian and Master of St John's College, Cambridge, died (1595)

5 François II, King of France and King Consort of Scotland, died (1560)

6 Sir Hugh Paulet, soldier and administrator, died (1573)

7 Henry Stuart, Lord Darnley and King of Scots, was born (1545)

8 Mary, Queen of Scots, was born (1542)

9 Hugh Ashton, Archdeacon of York, died (1522)

10 Thomas Culpeper, Gentleman of the Privy Chamber, and Francis Dereham, secretary to Katheryn Howard, were executed (1541)

11 Douglass Howard, Lady Sheffield, was buried (1608)

12 Anne of Denmark, Queen of Great Britain, was born (1574)

13 Francis Drake left Plymouth on the trip in which he circumnavigated the world (1577)

14 King James V of Scotland died (1542)

15 Sir Thomas Parry, Comptroller of the Household to Elizabeth I, died (1560)

16 Katharine of Aragon, Queen of England, was born (1485)

17 Matthew Parker was consecrated as Archbishop of Canterbury (1559)

18 Alexander, Duke of Ross, posthumous son of King James IV of Scotland, died (1515)

19 Katherine Palmer, Abbess of Syon, died in exile (1576)

20 Sir Francis Walsingham was appointed second Principal Secretary (1573)

21 Jasper Tudor, Earl of Pembroke and Duke of Bedford, died (1495)

22 Archbishop Warham resigned as Lord Chancellor (1514)

23 Sir Thomas Smith, scholar and diplomat, was born (1513)

24 Sir Thomas Cornwallis, Comptroller of the Household of Mary I, died (1604)

25 Lettice Knollys, Countess of Leicester, died (1634)

26 Rose Lok (Throckmorton), businesswoman, was born (1526)

27 Katherine Cooke, Lady Killigrew, died (1583)

28 Sir Nicholas Bacon, Lord Keeper of the Great Seal in Elizabeth I's reign, was born (1510)

29 George Clifford, 3rd Earl of Cumberland, was buried (1605)

30 Roger Ascham, scholar and tutor to Elizabeth I, died (1568)

31 The East India Company was granted a Royal charter (1600)

Birthdays	Anniversaries	Reminders	Projects

Gardening	Events	Occasions	Festivals

December

1   Maud Green, Lady Parr, died (1531)

2   **St Bibianus' Day**

Henry Howard, Earl of Surrey, was arrested and sent to the Tower of London (1546)

3   Sir Charles Brandon was given wardship and marriage of Elizabeth, Viscountess Lisle (1511)

4 **St Barbara's Day**

William Whitaker,
theologian and Master of St
John's College, Cambridge,
died (1595)

5 François II, King of France
and King Consort of
Scotland, died (1560)

6 **St Nicholas' Day**

Sir Hugh Paulet, soldier
and administrator, died
(1573)

December

7   **St Ambrose's Day**

Henry Stuart, Lord Darnley
and King of Scots, was born
(1545)

8   **Feast of the Conception of
the Blessed Virgin**

Mary, Queen of Scots, was
born (1542)

9   Hugh Ashton, Archdeacon
of York, died (1522)

10 Thomas Culpeper,
Gentleman of the Privy
Chamber, and Francis
Dereham, secretary to
Katheryn Howard, were
executed (1541)

11 **St Damasus' Day**

Douglass Howard, Lady
Sheffield, was buried (1608)

12 **St Columba's Day**

Anne of Denmark, Queen
of Great Britain, was born
(1574)

December

13 St Lucy's Day

Francis Drake left Plymouth
on the trip in which he
circumnavigated the world
(1577)

14 St Erkenwald's Day

King James V of Scotland
died (1542)

15

Sir Thomas Parry,
Comptroller of the
Household to Elizabeth I,
died (1560)

16 Katharine of Aragon,
Queen of England, was
born (1485)

17 Matthew Parker was
consecrated as Archbishop
of Canterbury (1559)

18 Alexander, Duke of Ross,
posthumous son of King
James IV of Scotland, died
(1515)

December

19 Katherine Palmer, Abbess
of Syon, died in exile (1576)

20 Sir Francis Walsingham was
appointed second Principal
Secretary (1573)

21 **St Thomas the Apostle's
Day**

Jasper Tudor, Earl of
Pembroke and Duke of
Bedford, died (1495)

22 **SS Cyril and Methodius' Day**

Archbishop Warham resigned as Lord Chancellor (1514)

23 Sir Thomas Smith, scholar and diplomat, was born (1513)

24 **Vigil of the Nativity of Christ**

Sir Thomas Cornwallis, Comptroller of the Household of Mary I, died (1604)

December

25 **Nativity of Christ (Christmas Day)**

Lettice Knollys, Countess of Leicester, died (1634)

26 **St Stephen's Day**

Rose Lok (Throckmorton), businesswoman, was born (1526)

27 **St John the Apostle's Day**

Katherine Cooke, Lady Killigrew, died (1583)

28 Feast of the Holy Innocents

Sir Nicholas Bacon, Lord Keeper of the Great Seal in Elizabeth I's reign, was born (1510)

29 St Thomas Becket's Day

George Clifford, 3rd Earl of Cumberland, was buried (1605)

30 Feast of King David

Roger Ascham, scholar and tutor to Elizabeth I, died (1568)

DECEMBER

31 The East India Company
was granted a Royal charter
(1600)

Notes

Notes

INDEX OF PEOPLE

Many people of the period did not use surnames, so are listed under their first name. Women are listed under their maiden names, as many married more than once. If their married name is well-known, it is added in brackets.

Adams, Clement (c. 1519 - 1587)
After graduating from King's College Cambridge, Adams joined the retinue of Prince Edward, as schoolmaster to the prince's companions. He wrote an account of Richard Chancellor's voyage to Moscow and produced an engraving of Sebastian Cabot's *mappa mundi*.

Alexander, Duke of Ross (1514 -1515)
The youngest son of James IV of Scotland and his wife, Margaret Tudor, Alexander was born seven months after the death of his father at the Battle of Flodden.

Anne of Cleves, Queen of England (1515 - 1557) Daughter of Duke John of Cleves, and Duchess Maria of Jülich-Berg, Anne was chosen to marry Henry VIII to cement an anti-Imperial alliance. Delighted with her portrait, Henry looked forward to the marriage, but found Anne unattractive in the flesh. An amicable annulment was arranged, and Anne remained in England, on good terms with Henry and his children.

Anne of Denmark, Queen of Great Britain (1574 - 1619) Anne was fifteen years old when she was married to James VI of Scotland. Three of the couple's children survived childhood: Henry, Prince of Wales (who died of typhoid fever at 18), Elizabeth, Queen of Bohemia, and Charles I. When James inherited the English throne, Anne became the first queen-consort of Great Britain. Through her patronage of the arts, she made the Jacobean court one of the most sophisticated in Europe.

Anne of York, Countess of Surrey (1475 - 1511) Anne was the third daughter of Edward IV and Elizabeth Woodville. In 1484, a marriage was arranged for Anne with Lord Thomas Howard, but this did not happen. The Howards supported Richard III and it took some time for the family to be rehabilitated following the Battle of Bosworth. Anne did marry Howard eventually and became Countess of Surrey.

Arthur, Prince of Wales (1486 - 1502)
The firstborn child of Henry VII and Elizabeth of York, Arthur was invested as Prince of Wales and sent to Ludlow Castle to preside over the Council of the Marches. In 1501, Arthur was married to the Spanish Princess, Katharine of Aragon, but died within six months of his wedding, to the grief of his parents and the whole country.

Arundell, Mary, Countess of Sussex and Arundel (c. 1474 - 1557) Daughter of Sir John Arundell of Lanherne, Cornwall, and his second wife, Katherine Grenville, Mary served at least two of Henry VIII's queens, Jane Seymour and Anne of Cleves, and his daughter, Mary. She married twice: Robert Radcliffe 1st Earl of Sussex by whom she had one son, Sir John Radcliffe; and then Henry FitzAlan, 19th Earl of Arundel.

Ascham, Roger (1515 - 1568) Ascham studied at St John's College, Cambridge, and lectured there in Greek. He was appointed Latin and Greek tutor to the Lady Elizabeth, despite opposition from her step-mother, Katherine Parr. Ascham was appointed Latin secretary to Mary I, then Elizabeth I. His most famous work was a treatise on archery, and another on Latin pedagogy entitled *The Schoolmaster*.

Ashmole, Elias (1617 - 1692) An antiquary, politician and astrologer, Ashmole was one of the founding Fellows of the Royal Society. He donated his substantial collection of artefacts, antiquarian library and priceless manuscripts to the University of Oxford where it forms the core of the Ashmolean Museum's collection.

Ashton, Hugh, Archdeacon of York (? - 1522) Ashton was closely associated with Lady Margaret Beaufort, Countess of Richmond and Derby. He was comptroller of her household and assisted with the foundation of her two Cambridge colleges (Christ's and St John's). He was also one of the executors of her will.

Bacon, Sir Francis (1561 - 1626) The son of Sir Nicholas Bacon, and Anne Cooke, Francis studied at Trinity College, Cambridge from the age of twelve. He enrolled at Gray's Inn and combined legal studies with diplomacy in the train of Sir Amyas Paulet, Ambassador to France. James VI & I appointed him Attorney General and then Lord Chancellor. Dismissed from office on charges of corruption, Bacon spent his later years writing works of philosophy, jurisprudence and science.

Bacon, Sir Nicholas (1510 - 1579) A courtier and politician, Sir Nicholas was a graduate of Corpus Christi College, Cambridge and Lord Keeper of the Great Seal for Elizabeth I. His second wife, Anne Cooke, author and scholar, was the sister-in-law of Sir William Cecil.

Barnham, Alice, Viscountess St Albans (1592 - 1650) Alice Barnham was just fourteen when she became the second wife of 45-year old Sir Francis Bacon. They had no children and within two weeks of his death she married John Underhill, with whom she had been rumoured to have being having an affair.

Bastard, Reverend Thomas (1566 - 1618) A Dorset clergyman best known for his epigrams, Bastard attended Winchester College and then New College, Oxford. His seven books of epigrams, *Chrestoleros*, was published in 1598.

Baffin, William (c. 1584 - 1622) Baffin took part in numerous voyages of exploration, including one that discovered the North-West Passage. He made detailed charts of the Red Sea and Persian Gulf. Baffin was killed in a skirmish with Portuguese ships in Oman. Baffin Bay and Baffin Island are both named after him.

Beaton, Cardinal David (c. 1494 - 1546) Archbishop of St Andrews and minister to James V of Scotland, Beaton led the pro-French faction in the early reign of Mary, Queen of Scots, before being assassinated by Protestant sympathisers in the wake of the burning of George Wishart.

Beaufort, Joan, Lady Howth (1433 - 1518) Daughter of Edmund Beaufort, 1st Duke of Somerset and Lady Eleanor Beauchamp, Joan was a cousin of Lady Margaret Beaufort. Her first marriage was to Robert St Lawrence, 3rd Baron Howth, a leading figure in fifteenth century Ireland, holding variously the offices of Chancellor of the Exchequer of Ireland and Lord Chancellor of Ireland. Widowed around 1483, Joan remarried Sir Richard Fry.

Beaufort, Lady Margaret, Countess of Richmond and Derby (1443 - 1509) Daughter of John, Duke of Somerset and Margaret Beauchamp of Bletsoe, Margaret was married, aged twelve, to Edmund Tudor, Earl of Richmond, half-brother of Henry VI. She was widowed whilst pregnant with her only child, Henry. Margaret married twice more, to Sir Henry Stafford, and then Lord Thomas Stanley, an adherent of Edward IV. On Henry Tudor's victory at the Battle of Bosworth in 1485, Margaret assumed a position of power and influence until her death in 1509.

Blagrave, Sir John (before 1560 - 1611) Blagrave, a mathematician, was a land surveyor and one of the first to draw estate maps to scale. Educated at Reading School and St John's College, Oxford, he designed and made instruments, including an astrolabe and sundials. Blagrave published four mathematical works, including *The Mathematical Jewel* (1585) and *Astrolabium Uranicum Generale* (1596).

Bodley, Sir Thomas (1545 - 1613)
A Fellow of Merton College, Oxford, and a Member of Parliament, Bodley was sent on several diplomatic missions for Elizabeth I's government. He is most famous for the re-founding of the library at Oxford, later re-named the Bodleian.

Boleyn, Anne, Queen of England (c. 1501 - 1536) Daughter of Sir Thomas Boleyn, a diplomat at Henry VIII's court, and Lady Elizabeth Howard, sister of the Duke of Norfolk, Anne's long love affair with Henry VIII changed the course of English history. Unable to procure an annulment of his first marriage to Katharine of Aragon, Henry eventually threw off Papal authority and the couple married secretly in January 1533, when Anne was a few weeks pregnant with a daughter, who would become Elizabeth I. Anne was executed on, almost certainly false, charges of adultery incest and treason, three years after she married Henry.

Boleyn, Sir Thomas, Earl of Wiltshire and Ormonde (c 1477 - 1539) Boleyn, an Ambassador for Henry VIII, was the father of Mary, Anne and George Boleyn and thus, briefly father-in-law to Henry VIII, and grandfather to Elizabeth I.

Borough, William (c.1536 - 1598)
An explorer and naval officer, Borough was Comptroller of the Navy. He sailed with his older brother and uncle on voyages, including one to explore the coast of Russia. Borough sailed and participated in the British attack on Cadiz in 1587. He was indicted for mutiny and cowardice but later acquitted.

Brandon, Lady Eleanor, Countess of Cumberland (1519 - 1547) The younger daughter of Mary, the French Queen, and Charles Brandon, Duke of Suffolk, Eleanor married Henry Clifford, 2nd Earl of Cumberland. Eleanor's place in the succession improved significantly with the passing of the Third Succession Act in 1544 which gave precedence to the descendants of Henry VIII's younger sister, Mary, over those of his older sister, Margaret. Eleanor died within nine months of her uncle, and her daughter, Lady Margaret Clifford, took her place in the order of succession.

Brandon, Lord Henry (1516 - 1522)
Brandon was the first son of Mary, the French Queen and Charles Brandon, Duke of Suffolk. For all his short life, he was Henry VIII's closest English male heir.

Bray, Sir Reginald (c. 1440 - 1503) A member of the household of Sir Henry Stafford, husband of Lady Margaret Beaufort, Countess of Richmond, Bray remained in her service following Stafford's death. Attainted for his part in Buckingham's rebellion, Bray escaped to France where he joined Lady Margaret's son, Henry Tudor. Once Henry became king, Bray became Chancellor of the Duchy of Lancaster and was one of Henry's most trusted councillors, acting as executor of his will.

Bryan, Sir Francis (c. 1490 - 1550) Known as the 'Vicar of Hell' for his rakish lifestyle, Bryan was a close associate and friend of Henry VIII throughout the king's life. A cousin of both Anne Boleyn and Jane Seymour, he initially favoured the Boleyn marriage, but was willing to work with Cromwell to replace Anne with Jane. Edward VI appointed him Lord Chief Justice of Ireland.

Bulkeley, Bishop Arthur (c. 1495 - 1553) Bulkeley, of a gentry family in Anglesey, was the first resident bishop of Bangor, and the first Welsh incumbent, since 1418. He was a Reformer, but a moderate one, who ordered teaching of Pater Noster, Creed, Ave and Ten Commandments to be in Welsh or English, depending on the preference of the congregation.

Bull, John (c 1562 - 1628) A composer, musician and organ builder renowned for his performances on the keyboard, Bull was one of the group known as the School of English Virginalists.

Burbage, Richard (1567 - 1619)
Burbage was one of the leading stage actors of the Elizabethan age. An associate of William Shakespeare, he was the star of the Lord Chamberlain's Men and played the title role in many of Shakespeare's plays.

Burgh, Sir John (1562 - 1594) A younger son of 4th Lord Burgh of Gainsborough, Burgh was a naval commander appointed by Sir Walter Raleigh to command the *Roebuck*. He died from a rapier wound suffered in a duel with Raleigh's stepbrother, John Gilbert.

Butts, Sir William (c. 1485 - 1545) One of Henry VIII's most important physicians, he treated Anne Boleyn for the sweating sickness in 1528 and was also the recipient of Henry's confidences in 1539 when the king confessed that, although he could not consummate his marriage to Anne of Cleves, he had 'nocturnal emissions' that proved his virility. This evidence was key in the annulment case.

Carey, Sir Henry, 1st Baron Hunsdon (1526 - 1596) Son of William Carey and Mary Boleyn, Hunsdon was a favourite of his first cousin, Elizabeth I, holding senior positions at her court. He was a Knight of the Garter and a Privy Councillor. Carey was also patron of William Shakespeare's playing company, the Lord Chamberlain's Men.

Carey, Katherine, Countess of Nottingham (1547 - 1603) Daughter of Elizabeth I's cousin, Henry Carey, 1st Baron Hunsdon, Katherine married Charles Howard, later 2nd Baron Howard of Effingham, Lord High Admiral of England and 1st Earl of Nottingham. They had five children. Katherine served Elizabeth I for 45 years and her death on 25 February 1603 was a great blow to Elizabeth, who died a month later.

Cavendish, Elizabeth (1555 - 1582)
Daughter of Sir William Cavendish and Bess of Hardwick, one of the wealthiest women of the Tudor period, Elizabeth married Charles Stuart, 1st Earl of Lennox, younger brother of Henry Stuart, Lord Darnley, without

the necessary royal permission, incurring Elizabeth I's wrath.

Charles V, Holy Roman Emperor (1500 - 1556) Charles ruled the largest expanse of territory since Charlemagne. He was Duke of Burgundy, King of Spain, and Emperor. His life was one of unremitting struggle to hold his disparate inheritance together, and fend off the existential threat to the Empire of Protestantism.

Cicely of York, Viscountess Welles (1469 - 1507) Cicely was the daughter of Edward IV and Elizabeth Woodville, and sister to Elizabeth of York and 'the Princes in the Tower'. Following the death of her husband, John, 1st Viscount Welles, Cicely scandalised the court by marrying Thomas Kyme, a lowly squire.

Clerk, John, Bishop of Bath and Wells (c. 1481 - 1541) Originally a protégé of Cardinal Wolsey, Clerk was appointed as Counsel to Katharine of Aragon during the annulment proceedings. He gave her little support, and later denied the validity of her marriage. Clerk continued to serve Henry VIII on diplomatic missions, including that which resulted in his marriage to Anne of Cleves.

Clifford, Lady Anne, 14th Baroness de Clifford (1590 - 1676) Daughter of the Earl of Cumberland, Lady Anne was a notable supporter of Jacobean literature. She married the Earl of Dorset, but despite the birth of five children, the couple were deeply unhappy. Unable to inherit her father's earldom, Lady Anne, recognised as Baroness Clifford, fought to obtain her father's estates. Her rights were finally recognised in 1643. Her second marriage, to the Earl of Pembroke and Montgomery, was also unhappy.

Coverdale, Miles (1488 - 1569) A graduate of Cambridge, Coverdale became an Augustinian Canon at Cambridge, under the Prior, Robert Barnes, an early advocate of religious reform. Coverdale spent seven years in Europe, probably assisting Tyndale in his Biblical translation. In 1538, Coverdale was appointed to oversee the printing of an approved translation of the Bible into English. After a further period of exile, he became Bishop of Exeter under Edward VI. Exiled again, he joined the Geneva circle, returning to England in 1559.

Cranmer, Thomas, Archbishop of Canterbury (1489 - 1556) Consecrated Archbishop of Canterbury in 1533, Cranmer declared Henry VIII's first marriage null. Under Edward VI, Cranmer moved further towards Protestantism and wrote the Liturgy and Book of Common Prayer which are still the foundation of the Church of England. He was burned for heresy under Mary I in 1556.

Cromwell, Gregory, 1st Baron Cromwell (c. 1520 - 1551) Gregory was the only surviving child of Thomas Cromwell. In 1537 he married Elizabeth Seymour, widowed sister of Jane Seymour, and thus became brother-in-law to the king. Gregory managed to escape any association with his father's arrest and execution. He was later granted a barony in his own right, and summoned to Parliament.

Cromwell, Thomas, 1st Earl of Essex (c. 1485 - 1540) Son of a small trader in Putney, Thomas Cromwell rose to become Henry VIII's chief minister. Although initially a supporter of the new queen, Anne Boleyn, he was involved in her downfall, whether of his own initiative or under order of the king. Cromwell lost the king's support in 1540 after promoting a disastrous marriage between Henry VIII and Anne of Cleves. He was accused of treason and beheaded.

de la Pole, Edmund, 3rd Duke of Suffolk (1471 - 1513) Edmund was the nephew of Edward IV and Richard III, and became the leading York claimant to the throne. He left England without permission in 1501 for the court of the Holy Roman Emperor, Maximilian. In 1506 Maximilian's son, Philip the Fair of Burgundy and his wife, Juana of Castile, were shipwrecked in

England. Henry VII made it clear that they could not leave until Suffolk returned. Maximilian agreed, on the promise that Suffolk's life would be spared. Henry VII kept his word and imprisoned Suffolk in the Tower of London. However, when Henry VIII was preparing for war in France in 1513, Suffolk was executed.

Denny, Sir Anthony (1501 - 1549) A trusted companion of Henry VIII during the king's last years, it was Denny who warned the king that death was imminent. A reformer, and an ally of Edward Seymour, he was appointed as Keeper of Westminster Palace under Edward VI.

Devereux, Frances, Duchess of Somerset (1599 - 1674) Daughter of Robert Devereux, 2nd Earl of Essex, and Frances Walsingham, Frances was not yet two when her father was executed for treason. She became the second wife of William Seymour, 2nd Duke of Somerset, grandson of Lady Katherine Grey, following the death of his first wife, Arbella Stuart. Frances and William had seven children and their descendants include HM The Queen; Diana, Princess of Wales and Sarah, Duchess of York.

Devereux, Lady Penelope, Lady Rich (1563 - 1607) Daughter of Elizabeth I's cousin, Lettice Knollys, Lady Penelope was the muse of Sir Philip Sidney, before marrying Lord Rich. She and Rich had several children, before she began a long-term affair with Charles Blount, Lord Mountjoy. Well-thought of at the court of James VI & I and Anne of Denmark, she forfeited royal favour when, after being granted a divorce from Rich, she married Mountjoy, defying the ruling of the Archbishop of Canterbury.

Devereux, Robert, 2nd Earl of Essex (1565 - 1601) Son of Walter Devereux and Lettice Knollys, Essex became the step-son of Elizabeth I's favourite, Robert Dudley, Earl of Leicester, when his mother re-married. Essex married Frances Walsingham, the daughter of Elizabeth I's spymaster, Sir Francis Walsingham, and they had five children. Highly favoured by the queen following the death of Leicester, Essex, although brilliant and courageous, was also proud and quarrelsome. As Elizabeth aged, her court became riven by factions, largely led by Essex in opposition to the queen's new chief minister, Robert Cecil. Matters came to a head when Essex led an ill-fated rebellion against the queen and was executed for treason.

Donne, John (1572 - 1631) Son of English Catholic recusants, Donne studied at Oxford and entered Lincoln's Inn before joining the household of Sir Thomas Egerton, Lord Keeper of the Great Seal. A clandestine marriage led to financial difficulties, but Donne began to produce some of the most admired poetry of the age. Rejecting the Catholicism of his family, he was ordained in the Church of England in 1615, and became Dean of St Paul's.

Douglas, Archibald, 6th Earl of Angus (c. 1489 - 1557) Angus married Margaret Tudor, the widowed Queen of Scots – an act which outraged the rest of the Scots nobles. Their only child, Lady Margaret Douglas, was born in 1515. In 1526, Angus seized control of his stepson, James V, and dominated Scottish government, until James escaped. Once free, the king banished Angus, who spent 16 years in England at the court of his brother-in-law, Henry VIII. Following the death of Henry, he was reconciled with the Scottish Government, and he opposed the English in the Wars of the Rough Wooing.

Douglas, James, 4th Earl of Morton (c. 1516 - 1581) An enemy of Mary, Queen of Scots, he was a ringleader in the assassination of her secretary, Riccio. Morton was regent for James VI, but was executed when James reached his majority, for complicity in the murder of the king's father, Lord Darnley.

Drake, Sir Francis (c. 1540 - 1596) A sailor, explorer and privateer, Drake's daring exploits against Spanish shipping and naval towns, including the great port of Cadiz, made him famous. He circumnavigated the world in the *Pelican* (1577 – 1580). Drake was second-in-command of the English fleet against the Spanish Armada of 1588.

Dudley, John, 2nd Earl of Warwick (c. 1527 - 1554) Son and heir of John Dudley, Duke of Northumberland, Warwick married Anne Seymour, eldest daughter of the former Protector Somerset, as a gesture of reconciliation between their fathers. Warwick was one of the signatories of the letters patent that attempted to set Lady Jane Grey on the throne, and took arms against Mary Tudor, alongside his father. Both were taken prisoners at Cambridge – Warwick was condemned to death but he was reprieved and died shortly after his release from the Tower of London.

Dudley, Lady Mary, Lady Sidney (c 1530 - 1586) Daughter of John Dudley, Duke of Northumberland, Lord Protector to Edward VI, and sister of Robert Dudley, Earl of Leicester, Mary was a lady-in-waiting and close confidante of Elizabeth I. She married Sir Henry Sidney, and was mother to the poet Sir Philip Sidney and Mary Herbert, Countess of Pembroke.

Dudley, Robert, Earl of Leicester (c. 1533 - 1588) The fifth son of the Duke of Northumberland, Robert was well-educated by Protestant tutors and became a companion to the young Edward, Prince of Wales. He married Amy Robsart, daughter of a Norfolk gentleman, apparently for love. Robert was imprisoned following the attempt to enthrone his sister-in-law, Lady Jane Grey, but Queen Mary released him to serve in King Philip's army. On Elizabeth I's accession, Robert became Master of the Horse. Elizabeth appeared to be deeply in love with him, and Amy's mysterious death was rumoured to be murder. Elizabeth favoured him for the rest of his life, granting him the title of Earl of Leicester, and making him a Privy Councillor.

Edward V, King of England (1470 - 1483?) Edward V, son of Edward IV and Elizabeth Woodville, became king at the age of twelve, having spent most of his childhood at Ludlow Castle in the Welsh Marches, as nominal head of the Council of the Marches. On his father's sudden death, he set out for London but was intercepted by his paternal uncle, Richard, Duke of Gloucester, and taken to the Tower. In early June it was declared that his parents' marriage was invalid and that he was therefore illegitimate. His uncle took the crown as Richard III and Edward was last seen, together with his brother, Richard, Duke of York, in the Tower in the summer of 1483.

Edward VI, King of England (1537 - 1553) The longed-for male heir of Henry VIII and his third wife, Jane Seymour, Edward became king at the age of nine. He was an ardent Protestant and attempted to bequeath the crown to his equally Protestant cousin, Lady Jane Grey, ahead of his half-sisters, Mary and Elizabeth. His short reign ended with his early death, aged sixteen.

Elizabeth I, Queen of England (1533 - 1603) Elizabeth was the daughter of Henry VIII and his second wife, Anne Boleyn. Following the early deaths of her half-brother, Edward VI, and half-sister, Mary I, she succeeded as queen in 1558. Elizabeth was Queen of England for forty-five years, and her reign is seen by many as a golden era of exploration, relative (by sixteenth century standards) religious tolerance and the flowering of English literature.

Elizabeth of York (1466 - 1503) Eldest daughter of Edward IV and Elizabeth Woodville, the death of her father turned her world upside down. Her uncle, Richard of Gloucester, pronounced Elizabeth and her siblings illegitimate and seized the throne. The Lancastrian claimant, Henry, Earl of Richmond, swore to marry her if he became king. Following his coronation, they were married and lived together harmoniously for seventeen years, before Elizabeth's death in childbirth.

Elyot, Sir Thomas (c 1490 - 1546) An administrator and diplomat whose friendship

with Sir Thomas More probably limited his career. He was a successful scholar, with his books and writings held in high esteem by his Humanist contemporaries; his Latin dictionary was one of the earliest comprehensive dictionaries of its type.

Fawkes, Guy (1570 - 1606) An English Catholic recusant, Fawkes spent his youth fighting for Catholic Spain in the Eighty Years War with The Netherlands. Returning to England, he became involved with a plot to blow up king and Parliament and impose a Catholic-led government. Fawkes was found in the cellars below the Parliament chamber, with barrels of gunpowder. He and his fellow conspirators suffered agonising deaths.

Fitzgerald, Gerald, 8th Earl of Kildare (1456 - 1513) Appointed Lord Lieutenant of Ireland by Edward IV, Fitzgerald remained in position under Henry VII. At heart, he was a Yorkist and was present at the crowning of Lambert Simnel as Edward VI in Dublin Cathedral. Forgiven for his part in the Simnel affair, in 1494 he spent a brief period in the Tower when he was captured by Irish enemies and sent to London accused of treason. Henry VII reappointed him as Lord Deputy, in which post he continued until his death in 1513.

FitzGerald, Lady Joan, Countess of Desmond (c. 1514 - 1565) Daughter and heir-general of the Earl of Desmond, Lady Joan married James Butler, Earl of Ormond, once Anne Boleyn's suitor. Her second marriage was to the courtier, Sir Francis Bryan. Finally, she married her cousin, Gerald FitzGerald, Earl of Desmond. During her life, the long-running feud between the Butlers and the FitzGeralds was contained, but it flared up after her death.

Fitzroy, Henry, 1st Duke of Richmond and Duke of Somerset (1519 - 1536) Fitzroy was the illegitimate son of Henry VIII by Bessie Blount. As Duke of Richmond, he nominally headed the Council of the North. He was married, aged 14, to Mary Howard, the daughter of the Duke of Norfolk. Like his uncle Arthur, and his cousins, Henry and Charles Brandon, Fitzroy died in his mid-teens.

Fitzwilliam, William, 1st Earl of Southampton (1490 - 1542) Fitzwilliam spent much of his youth at Henry VII's court, as a companion to the young Prince Henry. He received several court positions when Henry VIII became king and was later Admiral of the Fleet. Fitzwilliam succeeded Thomas Cromwell as Lord Privy Seal and was instrumental in arranging the annulment of Henry VIII's marriage to Anne of Cleves.

François I, King of France (1499 - 1547) François inherited the French throne from his distant cousin, Louis XII. His whole reign was dedicated to promoting French power in Italy, and reducing the influence of his great rival, Emperor Charles V.

François II, King of France (1544 - 1560) François inherited the French throne at the age of fifteen. Married to Mary, Queen of Scots, his short reign was dominated by her Guise relatives. He died painfully of an abscess in the ear aged sixteen.

François, Duke of Anjou (1555 - 1554) A younger son of Henri II of France, François led a moderate group, the Politiques, in the Wars of Religion, and attempted to become the leader of the opposition to Spain's control of the Netherlands.

Gardiner, Stephen, Bishop of Winchester (1483 - 1555) A graduate of Trinity, Cambridge, Gardiner was appointed as Secretary to Thomas Wolsey in the 1520s, before becoming Secretary to the king. One of the leaders of the conservative faction at Henry VIII's court, Gardiner was imprisoned for most of Edward VI's reign, emerging from the Tower of London in 1553 to be appointed Lord Chancellor to Mary I.

Green, Maud, Lady Parr (1492 - 1531) The daughter of Sir Thomas Green, of Boughton and Green's Norton, Maud was co-heiress, with her sister, Anne, Lady Vaux, to her father's estate. She married Sir Thomas Parr

and they had three children who survived infancy: Katherine, Henry VIII's sixth wife; William, 1st Marquis of Northampton and 1st Earl of Essex; and Anne, Countess of Pembroke. A friend and favoured lady-in-waiting of Katharine of Aragon, Maud played a full part in court life prior to Katherine's banishment. She accompanied the royal party to the Field of Cloth of Gold in 1520.

Grey, Henry, Duke of Suffolk (1517 - 1554) A descendant of Elizabeth Woodville's first marriage, Henry Grey married his distant cousin, Lady Frances Brandon, and thus became Henry VIII's nephew-by-marriage. A vigorous promoter of the Reformed Faith, he ensured his daughters, particularly the eldest, Lady Jane, were brought up according to its tenets. He and the Duke of Northumberland were instrumental in the effort to enthrone Lady Jane in 1553. Pardoned, at the intercession of his wife, he rebelled again, and was executed.

Henry, Duke of Cornwall (1511- 1511) The first-born son of Henry VIII and Katharine of Aragon, his birth was marked with a splendid joust, and his death a few weeks later with the most expensive ceremony of Henry VIII's reign. He is buried in the Henry VII Chapel at Westminster Abbey.

Henry VII, King of England (1457 - 1509) Descended through his grandmother, Katherine of Valois, from the French kings, and through his mother, Lady Margaret Beaufort, from Edward III, most of Henry's youth was spent in exile, as the last remnant of the House of Lancaster. He led a successful invasion of England in 1485, and, winning the crown in battle, became the first monarch of the Tudor dynasty.

Henry VIII, King of England (1491 - 1547) The second son of Henry VII and Elizabeth of York, Henry began his reign in traditional fashion, promoting war with France and expressing strong support for papal authority. By the late 1520s however, a combination of dynastic fears and his passion for Anne Boleyn, led him to request Pope Clement

VII to grant an annulment of his marriage to Katharine of Aragon. When it was not forthcoming, he broke with Rome, took the title Supreme Head of the Church in England and pursued a policy of ruthless repression of all dissent. Henry married a total of six times, but still left a minor heir, a disputed succession, and a country that was almost bankrupt despite the huge injection of cash from the Dissolution of the Monasteries.

Howard, Henry, Earl of Surrey (c. 1517 - 1547) Son of Thomas Howard, 3rd Duke of Norfolk, and Lady Elizabeth Stafford, Surrey was a first cousin of two of Henry VIII's wives - Anne Boleyn and Katheryn Howard. He was brought up with the king's illegitimate son, Henry Fitzroy. An extremely gifted poet, Surrey introduced the rhyming schema now associated with Shakespearian sonnets. He was convicted of treason and executed on rather dubious grounds relating to his armorial bearings.

Howard, Katheryn, Queen of England (c. 1521 - 1542) The fifth wife of Henry VIII, Katheryn was no more than 20, when she married the 49-year-old king. The daughter of Lord Edmund Howard, a younger son of Thomas Howard, 2nd Duke of Norfolk, and Joyce Culpeper, she was a first cousin of Anne Boleyn. Katheryn was executed for alleged adultery within two years of her marriage to Henry.

Howard, Thomas, 4th Duke of Norfolk (1536 - 1572) Son of Henry Howard, Earl of Surrey, Thomas inherited the dukedom of Norfolk from his grandfather. In the late 1560s, a marriage between Norfolk and Mary, Queen of Scots was mooted. Whilst it had widespread support amongst her councillors, Elizabeth I was furious when she discovered the plan, and Norfolk was imprisoned. Released, he became entangled in the Ridolfi Plot to replace Elizabeth with Mary and was executed for treason.

Howard, Lord William (c. 1510 - 1573) Half-brother of Thomas Howard, 3rd Duke of Norfolk, Howard was a prominent courtier

throughout his life. He deputised as Earl Marshal at the coronation of his niece, Anne Boleyn, and held the canopy over Elizabeth I at her baptism. He was imprisoned, but later pardoned, after the fall of Katheryn Howard, and took part in the Wars of the Rough Wooing. Supporting Mary I against Lady Jane Grey and then Wyatt, he was rewarded with the post of Lord Admiral.

James IV, King of Scots (1473 - 1513) James IV was one of Scotland's most successful kings, prior to his untimely death at the Battle of Flodden, where his army was routed by the English. He married Margaret Tudor, daughter of Henry VII of England, and their great-grandson, James VI & I, was the first monarch to rule both England and Scotland.

James V, King of Scots (1512 - 1542) James V sought to impose his authority after a troubled minority, during which his uncle, Henry VIII of England, attempted to destabilise his government. He had three children with his second wife, Marie of Guise, of which only one, Mary, survived him. James, having made huge progress, died aged thirty. He was a great Renaissance prince – enhancing Scottish castles in French-Renaissance style.

James VI & I, King of Great Britain (1566 - 1625) Son of Mary, Queen of Scots and Henry Stuart, Lord Darnley, James became King of Scotland at just over a year old when the Scottish nobles forced his mother to abdicate. He became the first monarch of a united Scotland, England and Ireland (Great Britain) in March 1603 when Elizabeth I died.

Jones, Inigo (1573 - 1652) An architect and theatre designer, Jones spent most of his formative years in Italy. He introduced the classical architecture of the Italian Renaissance to Britain with examples such as the Queen's House, Greenwich; Banqueting House, Whitehall; St Paul's, Covent Garden; and Covent Garden square. Jones came to the attention of the court of James VI & I as a designer of costumes and stage settings, under the patronage of Anne of Denmark. He collaborated with the playwright and actor, Ben Jonson, for many years.

Katharine of Aragon, Queen of England (1485 - 1536) The youngest daughter of Ferdinand of Aragon and Isabella of Castile, Katharine was the widow of Arthur, Prince of Wales, when she married his younger brother, Henry, in 1509. Only one of their children, later to become Mary I, survived more than a few weeks. Katharine was married to Henry for 24 years before Archbishop Cranmer ruled that their marriage was invalid and Katharine was merely Princess Dowager of Wales. Katherine fought vigorously for her marriage and refused to accept Cranmer's verdict. Sent to isolated castles and parted from her daughter, Katharine died at Kimbolton Castle, aged 51.

Katherine of York, Countess of Devon (1479 - 1527) The fifth daughter of Edward IV and Elizabeth Woodville, when her older sister, Elizabeth of York, became Henry VII's queen, Katherine was a member of her household. She was 20 when she married William Courtenay, Earl of Devon. Although he came under suspicion of treason and was imprisoned, Katherine herself remained free. She had two children, Margaret and Henry. When her nephew, Henry VIII, inherited the throne she was one of the most important court ladies, and stood godmother to his daughter, Mary.

Kett, Francis (c. 1547- 1589) Nephew of Robert Kett, leader of Kett's Rebellion, Francis was a Fellow of Corpus Christi, Cambridge. He published various religious treatises, including *The Glorious and Beautiful Garland of Man's Glorification, containing the godly mistery of heavenly Jerusalem*. He also practised medicine. An Anglican minister, he was burned for denying the Divinity of Christ.

Kingston, Sir William (c. 1476 - 1540) Kingston served in military and diplomatic missions in the period 1500 – 1524 before

being appointed as Constable of the Tower. In that capacity he had the unenviable job of arresting Wolsey, guarding Sir Thomas More, Bishop John Fisher and Anne Boleyn, and eventually, Thomas Cromwell.

Louis XII, King of France (1462 - 1515) Louis inherited the throne from his distant cousin, and brother-in-law, Charles VIII. In retaliation for Henry VIII's invasion of France in 1513, Louis recognised Richard de la Pole as the rightful king of England. In the treaty which ended Henry's war in France, Louis was married to Mary, younger daughter of Henry VII, dying, apparently of exhaustion, within three months.

Margaret of York, Duchess of Burgundy (1446 - 1503) Margaret was the devoted sister of Edward IV and Richard III. Married to Charles the Bold, Duke of Burgundy, as his third wife, she had no children but was on good terms with her stepdaughter, Mary. Following Charles's death, Margaret gave support to the new duchess and was on good terms with Mary's husband, Maximilian, King of the Romans. Once Henry VII took the crown, Margaret was an inveterate supporter of Yorkist plots; she claimed to recognise Perkin Warbeck as her nephew and gave him unstinting support.

Margaret Tudor, Queen of Scots (1489 - 1541) Eldest daughter of Henry VII and Elizabeth of York, Margaret married James IV of Scotland to seal the Treaty of Perpetual Peace in 1503. Of her four children with James, only one, James V, survived childhood. Margaret's daughter by her second husband, the 6th Earl of Angus, Lady Margaret Douglas, was both aunt and mother-in-law of Mary, Queen of Scots. Margaret's descendants have reigned in England and Scotland since 1603.

Marie of Guise, Queen and Regent of Scots (1515 - 1560) A member of the powerful house of Guise-Lorraine, Marie married the Duke of Longueville, then, widowed, rejected Henry VIII in favour of James V of Scotland. She acted as regent for her daughter, Mary, Queen of Scots, but died in the middle of a war between the Protestant and Catholic factions in Scotland.

Marlowe, Christopher (1564 - 1593) Born in Canterbury and educated at the King's School, Marlowe won a scholarship to Corpus Christi, Cambridge. After graduation, he began his career as a poet and playwright, producing some of the most notable works of the age: *Dido, Queen of Carthage*; *Doctor Faustus*, and *The Jew of Malta* are among his most famous works. Marlowe also had a parallel career in the Elizabethan secret service. He is believed to have been killed in a tavern brawl in Deptford in 1593, although the circumstances are fraught with mystery.

Mary I, Queen of England (1516 - 1558) Daughter of Henry VIII and his first wife, Katharine of Aragon, Mary became England's first queen-regnant in 1553. She sought to re-impose Catholicism following the brief reign of her Protestant half-brother, Edward VI, but died at the age of 42, after a reign of only five years and was succeeded by her Protestant half-sister, Elizabeth I.

Mary, Queen of France, Duchess of Suffolk (1496 - 1533) Mary Tudor, daughter of Henry VII and Elizabeth of York, was briefly married to the much older Louis XII of France. She secretly married Charles Brandon, 1st Duke of Suffolk, much to her brother, Henry VIII's, ire. Their eldest daughter, Lady Frances Brandon, was the mother of Lady Jane Grey.

Mary, Queen of Scots and Queen of France (1542 - 1587) Daughter of James V and Marie of Guise, Mary was six days old when her father died, and she inherited his throne. Engaged to the Dauphin and sent to live at the French court at the age of five, the widowed Mary returned to Scotland thirteen years later. Mary was the first queen-regnant in the British Isles and her reign was marked by religious and political rivalry between the pro-English Protestant party and the pro-French Catholic party. Mary was deposed in 1568, and subsequently imprisoned in England until her execution in 1587 for involvement in a plot against Elizabeth I of England.

Morton, John, Archbishop of Canterbury (c. 1420 - 1500) A member of Edward IV's Council, Morton was involved in the Duke of Buckingham's rebellion, and was attainted by Parliament. His support for Henry Tudor was an important factor in the latter's successful bid for the throne. Under Henry VII he became Archbishop of Canterbury, and Lord Chancellor.

Neville, Cicely, Duchess of York (1415 - 1495) Cicely was the youngest child of Ralph Neville, 1st Earl of Westmorland and Joan Beaufort, daughter of John of Gaunt, Duke of Lancaster. She was married at the age of 14 to her father's ward, Richard, Duke of York, who became one of the key protagonists of the Wars of the Roses. On the accession of her son as Edward IV, Cicely, became a prominent figure at court.

Neville Anne, Queen of England (1456 - 1485) Daughter of Richard Neville, Earl of Warwick, also known as 'Warwick the Kingmaker', Anne was first the wife of Prince Edward of Lancaster, then of Richard, Duke of Gloucester, later Richard III. Anne lost her only son, and the grief probably contributed to her early death.

Oughtred, William (1575 - 1660) Educated at Eton College and King's College Cambridge, Oughtred was an Anglican minister and mathematician who invented the slide rule and introduced the symbols for multiplication and proportion, and the abbreviations for the sine and cosine functions.

Parr, Katherine, Queen of England (1512 - 1548) The sixth and last wife of Henry VIII, Katherine had been married and widowed twice before she married the king. She built close relationships with all three of Henry's children. She caused some scandal by marrying Sir Thomas Seymour within months of Henry's death. Katherine's happiness was short lived, however, as she died of puerperal fever following the birth of her first child, Mary Seymour.

Philip II, King of Spain, Duke of Burgundy (1527 - 1598) Philip inherited Spain as well as The Netherlands from his father, Emperor Charles V. Whilst he eventually brought the Italian Wars to an end with the Treaty of Cateau-Cambrèsis, much of his life was devoted to protecting Catholicism in Europe and trying to maintain control of the Netherlands. The Armada he sent against England in 1588 failed, undermining his control of the Spanish territories in the New World.

Plantagenet, Arthur, Viscount Lisle (? - 1542) Lisle was the illegitimate son of Edward IV and thus half-brother to Elizabeth of York and uncle to Henry VIII. Arrested for treason when Lord Deputy of Calais, Lisle spent two years in the Tower of London. On learning the news of his release, he had a heart attack and died.

Pocahontas (c 1596 - 1617) Captured by the English during the Anglo-Indian conflicts in Virginia in the early seventeenth century, Pocahontas converted to Christianity and married John Rolfe. She came to England with her husband in 1616 and was fêted in London court circles.

Pole, Henry, 1st Baron Montagu (c. 1492 - 1539) The oldest son and heir of Margaret, Countess of Salisbury, he was on good terms with his cousin Henry VIII until his father-in-law, Edward Stafford, 3rd Duke of Buckingham, was executed for treason. Montagu supported Henry's annulment of his first marriage, but by the late 1530s the king was becoming increasingly suspicious of Montagu and their mutual cousin, the Marquis of Exeter. Montagu was accused of treason and executed.

Pole, Katherine, Countess of Huntingdon (1511 - 1571) Daughter of Henry, Lord Montagu, and granddaughter of Margaret, Countess of Salisbury, Katherine was probably an attendant on Princess Mary from 1525. She married Francis Hastings, Earl of Huntingdon in 1532. The couple had eleven children. Francis was sent to the Tower for supporting Lady Jane Grey. Katherine's uncle, however, was Cardinal Pole, the last Catholic Archbishop of Canterbury, and Katherine herself was 'restored in blood' by Mary I.

Pole, Lady Margaret, Countess of Salisbury (1473 - 1541) Daughter of George, Duke of Clarence and Isabella Neville, Margaret was the niece of Edward IV and first cousin to Elizabeth of York. Her husband, Sir Richard Pole, was a half-nephew of Margaret Beaufort. A close friend of Katharine of Aragon, she was godmother and Lady Governess to Katharine's daughter, Mary. Her hereditary title of Countess of Salisbury was restored in 1512. Margaret and her sons were suspected of treason during the Exeter Conspiracy. She was arrested in 1538 and imprisoned in the Tower, until 1541, when she was executed in a botched beheading.

Pole, Cardinal Reginald (1500 - 1558) Son of Lady Margaret and Sir Richard Pole, Reginald's education was initially paid for by Henry VIII, until his support for the papacy, combined with his nearness to the throne, rendered him one of Henry's deadliest enemies. In 1538 Pole's brother, mother and cousin were arrested and imprisoned on charges of treason and two of them later executed. In 1556 Pole was ordained priest and became the last Catholic Archbishop of Canterbury, under Mary I.

Pole, Ursula, Lady Stafford (c. 1498 - 1570) The only daughter of Margaret, Countess of Salisbury, in 1519 Ursula married the oldest son of the Duke of Buckingham. Unfortunately, Ursula's father-in-law, Edward Stafford, 3rd Duke of Buckingham, was executed in 1521. Ursula's husband was restored to a barony in 1547. Like many other families, Ursula's was divided by religion: her brother, Reginald, was the last Catholic Archbishop of Canterbury, her daughter, Dorothy, was in exile in Geneva during his tenure with other radical Protestants and her son, Thomas, was executed in 1557 for an attempt on the throne.

Pope, Sir Thomas (c.1507 - 1559)
Pope trained as a lawyer, and was friends with Thomas Audley, later Lord Chancellor. He became an officer of the Court of Augmentations, which enabled him to amass a fortune. Despite profiting from the Dissolution of the Monasteries, he was a religious conservative, and became a Privy Councillor under Mary I. He founded Trinity College, Oxford.

Poynings, Sir Edward (1459 - 1521)
Poynings was an early supporter of Henry, Earl of Richmond, joining him in exile in Brittany, and taking part in the invasion of England and victory at Bosworth in 1485. He was appointed Governor of Calais, and then Lord Deputy of Ireland. Under Henry VIII, he negotiated with Spain and the Empire for the alliance against France that culminated in the war of 1513.

Raleigh, Sir Walter (c. 1554 - 1618)
Raleigh studied at Oxford and fought in The Netherlands before taking part in an exploratory journey to the Americas with his half-brother, Humphrey Gilbert. Catching Elizabeth I's eye, he became Captain of her Guard before incurring her wrath by his secret marriage to Elizabeth Throckmorton. To regain favour, he set off on an expedition to find El Dorado and sponsored two attempts to found colonies in America. James VI & I disliked Raleigh, and he was found guilty of plotting the king's death. He spent twelve years in the Tower of London, working on his *History of the World*, before being released. Another voyage to find El Dorado failed and he was executed for interfering with Spanish shipping, against orders.

Riccio, David (c 1533 - 1566) Riccio, an Italian courtier and musician, became private secretary to Mary, Queen of Scots, much to the chagrin of her husband, Lord Darnley, and other leading Scottish nobles. Riccio was dragged from the pregnant Mary's presence, as she was restrained by Darnley, and stabbed to death, precipitating a series of events that resulted, ultimately, in Mary's abdication.

Rich, Sir Richard, 1st Baron Rich (c. 1496 - 1567) Rich has probably the worst reputation of any politician of the Tudor period - dishonest, rapacious, double-dealing, and a bearer of false witness. Appointed Solicitor-General in 1533, he acted as Cromwell's second in the Dissolution of the Monasteries. His (probably false) testimony was instrumental in the convictions of Sir Thomas More and Bishop John Fisher for treason. Rich turned against Cromwell and became associated with the conservative faction in religion, personally taking part in the racking of Anne Askew. He re-emerged as a reformer under Edward VI, whom he served as Lord Chancellor. Under Mary I he persecuted Protestants, before going on to advise Elizabeth I during the early part of her reign.

Richard III, King of England (1452 - 1485)
Richard was the youngest son of Richard, Duke of York, and Cicely Neville. Given the title of Duke of Gloucester, he was a loyal lieutenant to his brother, Edward IV. It was agreed that Richard would take the position of Lord Protector to his nephew, Edward V. But Richard announced that the marriage of Edward IV and Elizabeth Woodville had been invalid and that therefore Edward V and his siblings were illegitimate. Richard was crowned on 22nd June 1483 but there was widespread murmuring. On 22nd August 1485, Richard was defeated and killed at the Battle of Bosworth.

Robsart, Amy, Lady Dudley (1532 - 1560)
The daughter of a Norfolk gentleman, Amy's marriage to Lord Robert Dudley, son of the Duke of Northumberland, was probably a love-match as she was of much lower rank than her husband. Following Northumberland's attempt to put Lady Jane Grey on the throne, Robert was imprisoned. After his release, the couple lived quietly until the accession of Elizabeth I. Robert became the queen's Master of Horse, and it was soon rumoured that Elizabeth was in love with him. In 1560 Amy was found dead at the bottom of a staircase. The

circumstances of her death have never been fully explained.

Roe, Sir Thomas (1581 - 1644) After an early voyage to the Americas with Sir Walter Raleigh, Roe became ambassador for James VI & I at the courts of the Holy Roman Emperor, the Ottoman Sultan, and the Mughal Emperor. He wrote several books about his experiences in foreign courts. Late in his diplomatic life, he worked to affect a peace between Sweden and Poland, which greatly enhanced Protestant strength in the Thirty Years War. Roe last sat in the Long Parliament for the University of Oxford, but, after returning from a final diplomatic mission for Charles I, did not resume his seat.

Rouse, John (1574 - 1652) A graduate of Balliol College, and a Fellow of Oriel College, Oxford, Rouse became Bodley's Librarian in 1620. Rouse took the rules of the institution so seriously that he refused Charles I permission to borrow a volume.

Russell, Lady Anne, Countess of Warwick (c. 1548 - 1604) Daughter of Francis Russell, 2nd Earl of Bedford, Anne joined the court on Elizabeth I's accession, and five years later married Ambrose, Earl of Warwick, brother of Elizabeth's favourite, Lord Robert Dudley. Despite a significant age gap, and the failure of the marriage to produce children, the couple were happy. Anne became *'more beloved and in greater favour … than any other woman in the kingdom'* according to her niece, Lady Anne Clifford, and remained with Elizabeth until the queen's death.

Ruthven, Patrick, 3rd Lord Ruthven (c. 1520 - 1566) Lord Ruthven was one of the Lords of the Congregation who sought to depose the Catholic Regent of Scotland, Marie of Guise. In pursuit of this, he was a signatory to the Treaty of Berwick, which requested English aid. When Mary, Queen of Scots took up personal rule, he was appointed as a Privy Councillor, but she had a visceral antipathy toward him, and suspected he practised witchcraft. It was Ruthven who, although mortally ill, led the band of assassins who killed Mary's secretary, David Riccio, within earshot of the pregnant queen. He died in exile in England.

Sackville, Richard (1589 - 1624) Richard Sackville, 3rd Earl of Dorset, was married to Lady Anne Clifford, a patron of literature and literary figure in her own right. Dorset's gambling and infidelities, and Anne's constant litigation, made the marriage unhappy.

Sadler, Sir Ralph (1507 - 1587) Placed in the household of Thomas Cromwell as a child, Sadler began his career as Cromwell's secretary. He went on to hold senior positions in the service of four Tudor monarchs. He was an ambassador to Scotland and latterly, a reluctant gaoler of Mary, Queen of Scots.

Savile, Sir Henry (1549 - 1622) Savile was Warden of Merton College, Oxford, and Latin Secretary to Elizabeth I. He was a notable translator of the classics and early Christian texts. His best known individual translations were of *Tacitus*, and *St Chrysostum* but his most important work was as one of the committed which produced the *King James Bible* in 1611.

Scrope, John, 5th Baron Scrope of Bolton (c.1437 - 1498) A Yorkist, he fought for Richard III at the Battle of Bosworth, and then later supported Lambert Simnel's rebellion. He was pardoned, but incurred a heavy fine. The lenient treatment may reflect the fact that Scrope's wife, Elizabeth St John, was half-sister to Lady Margaret Beaufort, Henry VII's mother.

Seymour, Edward, Duke of Somerset (c. 1500 - 1552) Oldest brother of Jane Seymour, he was an accomplished military commander, and served Henry diligently in the War of the Rough Wooing with Scotland. Seymour quickly took power on Henry's death, overturning the provisions of Henry's will that envisaged a regency council. He implemented religious reform but, irritating the other councillors with his arrogance, he was ousted and eventually executed.

Seymour, Edward, Viscount Beauchamp and Earl of Hertford (1539 - 1621) Son of Lord Protector Somerset, he fell in love with Lady Katherine Grey, sister of the ill-fated Lady Jane. The two married in secret. When Elizabeth I discovered the match, the pair were sent to the Tower. Lady Katherine bore a son, and later, a second son, after the Lieutenant of the Tower allowed them to meet. They were separated and Katherine died young. Seymour made two more clandestine matches, but was eventually received back into royal favour.

Seymour, Elizabeth, Countess of Winchester (c 1518 - 1568) Elizabeth Seymour was the sister of Jane, third wife of Henry VIII, and aunt of Edward VI. Her first husband, Sir Anthony Ughtred, was Governor of Jersey; her second was Gregory Cromwell, son of Sir Thomas Cromwell; and her third husband, John Paulet, 2nd Marquis of Winchester, was Governor of the Isle of Wight.

Seymour, Jane, Queen of England (c.1508 - 1537) Probably a maid-of-honour to Katharine of Aragon, she then fulfilled the same role with Anne Boleyn. Henry VIII began courting Jane in late 1535 and married her within ten days of Anne's execution. Jane promoted reconciliation between Henry and his elder daughter, Mary, and was sympathetic to the aims of the rebels in the Pilgrimage of Grace. She died within a fortnight of giving birth to Henry's longed-for male heir.

Shakespeare, William (1564 - 1616) The most famous poet and playwright in the English language, Shakespeare performed in front of James VI & I and his wife, Anne of Denmark. Shakespeare was also an astute businessman and invested his profits in creating a comfortable life for his wife and family in his native Stratford-upon-Avon. His plays have influenced perceptions of history for over four hundred years.

Sheffield, Edmund, 1st Baron Sheffield (1521 - 1549) In his youth, Sheffield was a ward of George Boleyn, brother of Anne Boleyn, but on his execution, Sheffield's wardship was transferred to the Earl of Oxford, whose daughter he married. Lord Sheffield was part of the royal force sent to Norfolk to suppress Kett's Rebellion and was killed during the campaign.

Sidney, Sir Philip (1554 - 1586) The nephew of Elizabeth I's favourite, Robert Dudley, Earl of Leicester, Philip won praise for his intellect and his ability – although he displeased the queen when he criticised her proposed marriage to the Duke of Anjou. His most famous works are *The Countess of Pembroke's Arcadia*, dedicated to his sister, and *Stella and Astrophel,* sonnets which took Lady Penelope Devereux as his muse. A committed Protestant, he urged English support for the Protestant insurgents in The Netherlands, and died from wounds sustained at the Battle of Zutphen.

Skelton, John (c. 1460 - 1529) Probably educated at Cambridge, Skelton became a protégé of Lady Margaret Beaufort, Countess of Richmond and Derby. He was one of the tutors to her grandson, Henry VIII, and a court poet. Skelton was ordained around 1498 and in 1504 retired from court to his living in Norfolk. He continued to write biting satire, including the well-known attack on Cardinal Wolsey – *Why come ye not to court?*

Smith, Sir Thomas (1513 - 1577) A fellow of Queens' College, Cambridge, he lectured on Natural Philosophy and Greek. Smith took another degree at the University of Padua, and on his return, became friendly with John Cheke. Together, they transformed the study of Greek. Smith was appointed Regius Professor of Civil Law, then Vice-Chancellor of Queens' and Vice Chancellor of the University. He embraced the Reformation and acted as Secretary to Edward Seymour, Lord Protector. Dismissed from public life under Mary I, he returned to Parliament under Elizabeth I.

Southwell, Sir Richard (c. 1503 - 1564) Southwell first entered royal circles as tutor to Gregory Cromwell, son of Thomas. Subsequently, he served Henry VIII, Edward VI, Mary I and Elizabeth I in various roles - Privy Councillor, High Sheriff of Norfolk and Suffolk, and Master of the Armoury.

Southwell, Sir Robert (c. 1506 - 1559) Southwell trained as a lawyer, probably at Middle Temple. He married the heiress, Margaret Neville, and her family home became his main seat. Henry VIII requested the City of London to appoint him as Serjeant in 1535, and he became an MP the following year. He held various legal positions in the Court of Augmentations, then as Master of the Rolls. He supported Mary I during the succession crisis of 1553, and against Wyatt in 1554, and was well-rewarded.

Spenser, Edmund (c. 1552 – 1599) A graduate of Pembroke College, Cambridge, Spenser served in Elizabeth I's army in Ireland. Like many Elizabethans, he advocated total domination of Ireland, and lost his own home there during the war. Spenser wrote some of the most admired poems and prose in English, including *The Faerie Queen*, developing his own rhyming scheme. Elizabeth appreciated his verse, and paid him a pension.

Stanhope, Anne, Duchess of Somerset (c. 1497 - 1587) The second wife of Edward Seymour, Duke of Somerset, Anne probably served Katharine of Aragon, as well as her sister-in-law, Jane Seymour. Like her husband, Anne was a Reformer, and was suspected of involvement with Anne Askew, who was burnt for heresy. Nevertheless, she remained a friend of the Catholic Princess Mary. She discouraged her son's involvement with Lady Katherine Grey, and survived long into Elizabeth I's reign, having married her steward.

Stafford, Edward, 3rd Duke of Buckingham (1478 - 1521) The highest-ranking noble in England, Buckingham was descended from Edward III and had a realistic claim to be

the senior representative of the House of Lancaster. He was also Henry's first cousin once removed, being the son of Katherine Woodville. He was executed for treason in 1521.

Stanley, Henry, 4th Earl of Derby (1531 - 1593) Connected to much of the English nobility, Stanley was married to Lady Margaret Clifford, daughter of Henry VIII's niece, Lady Eleanor Brandon. A Privy Councillor to Elizabeth I and her ambassador to France, he took part in the trial of Mary, Queen of Scots, and later acted as Lord High Steward at the trial of Philip Howard, Earl of Arundel.

Stanley, Thomas, 1st Earl of Derby (1435 - 1504) Lord Thomas Stanley, hereditary King of Man, was one of the few nobles who managed never to fight a battle in the Wars of the Roses. Forced to choose, he became a follower of Edward IV, and was rewarded with marriage to the widowed Lady Margaret Beaufort. Ostensibly he supported Richard III, but he turned a blind eye to his wife's plans for an invasion by her son, Henry, Earl of Richmond. Whilst promising to back Henry, he failed to engage at Bosworth, although his brother's decisive move in support of Henry swung the battle in Henry's favour. As the new king's stepfather, Stanley received the Earldom of Derby – a title still enjoyed by his descendants.

Stanley, Sir William (c.1435 - 1495) Younger brother of Lord Thomas, he was a more active supporter of York, fighting for him at the Battle of Blore Heath, and for Edward IV at Towton and Tewkesbury, where he captured Marguerite of Anjou. He turned against Richard III, and played a decisive role in the Battle of Bosworth. For unknown reasons, he became embroiled with Perkin Warbeck, and was executed.

Stuart, Henry, Lord Darnley and King of Scots (1545 - 1567) The great-grandson of Henry VII, through his eldest daughter, Margaret, Darnley had a credible claim to the throne of England. He also had a more tenuous claim to that of Scotland, through his father, the Earl of Lennox. Darnley's mother schemed to arrange a match between Darnley and his cousin, Mary, Queen of Scots. The plan was successful but the marriage was a dismal failure. Darnley was assassinated in February 1567, and the resulting fall-out drove Mary from the throne, to be replaced by their son, James VI.

Stuart, Matthew, 4th Earl of Lennox (1516 - 1571) A Scots nobleman, married to Lady Margaret Douglas, the half-sister of James V, he was the father-in-law of Mary, Queen of Scots, and became regent for her son, James VI. Lennox was assassinated during the struggle for control between the Queen's Party and the King's Party, which supported the rival claims of Mary and James.

Tailboys, Sir Gilbert, 1st Baron Tailboys of Kyme (c. 1497 - 1530) Tailboys joined Wolsey's household, and the Cardinal probably arranged his marriage to Bessie Blount, mother of Henry VIII's illegitimate son, Henry Fitzroy. He sat in the 1529 Parliament, then was summoned to the Lords as Baron Tailboys. He and Elizabeth had three children, who all succeeded in the barony, but produced no grandchildren.

Talbot, George, 4th Earl of Shrewsbury and 4th Earl of Waterford (c. 1468 - 1538) An early supporter of the Tudors, Talbot fought for Henry at the Battle of Bosworth. He remained high in the new king's favour and was godfather to his eldest daughter, Margaret, later Queen of Scots. He supported Henry VIII in his annulment suit against Katharine of Aragon, swearing that he believed Katharine's marriage to Prince Arthur had been consummated. He played a significant part in containing the Pilgrimage of Grace.

Throckmorton, Elizabeth (Bess), Lady Raleigh (1565 - c. 1647) Daughter of Sir Nicholas, Elizabeth I's ambassador to Mary, Queen of Scots, Bess joined the court as a Gentlewoman of the Privy Chamber. She and Sir Walter Raleigh fell in love and married

without royal permission. The furious queen imprisoned them both, but had no grounds for her action, as neither had royal blood, so did not need her consent for their union. Sir Walter was eventually forgiven but Bess did not re-join the court. Raleigh was again imprisoned under James VI & I and eventually executed.

Teerlinc, Levina (? - 1576) Daughter of a Flemish miniaturist, she and her husband moved to England, where she obtained a post as a court painter, specialising in miniatures. She served both Mary I and Elizabeth I, but none of her apparently numerous works can be identified with absolute certainty.

Tilney, Elizabeth, Countess of Surrey (? - 1497) A Norfolk heiress, Elizabeth first married Sir Humphrey Bourchier, the great-great grandson of Edward III. Her second marriage was to the Earl of Surrey, later 2nd Duke of Norfolk. Her numerous descendants included the queens, Anne Boleyn and Katheryn Howard; Mary Boleyn; Sir Francis Bryan, Lord Lieutenant of Ireland; the poet, Henry Howard, Earl of Surrey; Mary Howard, wife of Henry VIII's illegitimate son; Thomas Fiennes, Baron Dacre of the South (executed following the Pilgrimage of Grace); Lettice Knollys, Countess of Leicester; Lady Penelope Devereux; Bess Throckmorton, Lady Raleigh; and Lady Frances Howard, Countess of Somerset.

Tresham, Sir Thomas (? - 1559) Tresham, whose first wife, Anne Parr, was a cousin of Henry VIII's sixth wife, Katherine Parr, was a prominent politician in the reigns of Henry VIII and Mary I. Tresham was one of the first to declare loyalty to Mary I when she took up arms to claim the crown, and accompanied her on her triumphant entry into London.

Tudor, Edmund, 1st Earl of Richmond (1430 - 1456) The eldest son of Katherine of Valois, Dowager Queen of England, and Owen Tudor, Edmund was granted titles and land by his half-brother, Henry VI, as well as the hand of Lady Margaret Beaufort, cousin to the king, and in the Lancastrian line of succession. He jostled for power in South Wales with William Herbert, a retainer of Richard of York, and died shortly after being besieged in Carmarthen Castle.

Tudor, Edmund, Duke of Somerset (1499 - 1500) The third son of Henry VII and Elizabeth of York, Edmund died aged about eighteen months. He was buried in Westminster Abbey, with the Duke of Buckingham acting as Chief Mourner.

Tudor, Jasper, Duke of Bedford (1431 - 1495) Jasper, the younger son of Katherine of Valois, and Owain Tudor, was ennobled by his half-brother, Henry VI. He was the most loyal Lancastrian of all, never once abandoning Henry VI, Marguerite of Anjou or their son, Prince Edward. After Edward of Lancaster's death, Jasper turned to his other nephew, Henry Tudor. He became the boy's greatest protector, went into exile with him in Brittany, and helped master-mind the successful invasion of England in 1485.

Tunstall, Cuthbert, Bishop of Durham (1474 - 1559) Tunstall wrote an influential mathematics primer, was a member of humanist circles, and one of Henry VIII's longest-serving councillors. He accepted the break with Rome, but remained conservative in religion. He continued in post throughout the reigns of Edward VI and Mary I but refused to take the renewed Oath of Supremacy under Elizabeth I. Imprisoned at Lambeth, he died within a few weeks.

Vives, Juan Luis (1493 - 1540) A native of Valencia, Vives held various roles at the court of Archduchess Marguerite in the Low Countries. He studied at the University of Paris, then took a Professorship at the University of Leuven. In England, he was Reader in Greek, Latin and Rhetoric at Wolsey's Cardinal College, Oxford. Vives was the first scholar to write a treatise promoting state assistance for the poor - *De Subventione Pauperum Sive de Humanis Necessitatibus*. He drew up a plan for the education of Princess Mary, but his support

for his patron, Katharine of Aragon, during the annulment proceedings, led to house arrest and a permanent departure to Bruges.

Walsingham, Sir Francis (c 1532 - 1590) Walsingham was a firm Protestant. He was Elizabeth I's ambassador to France where he witnessed the Massacre of St Bartholomew which convinced him that Elizabeth and England were vulnerable to Catholic plotting. Working with Lord Burghley, he set up a comprehensive espionage system which concentrated on identifying Catholic plotters. His patient work led to the uncovering of the Babington Plot to replace Elizabeth with Mary, Queen of Scots – although he probably had a hand in inciting the conspiracy.

Warbeck, Perkin (c. 1474 - 1499) Perkin Warbeck claimed to be Richard, Duke of York, younger son of Edward IV. He was supported in his claims by all those who wished to unseat Henry VII. After several years of attempted invasions, Warbeck was captured, and held under house arrest in Henry's own palace, before a further attempt to stir rebellion resulted in despatch to the Tower of London. In 1499, he was executed, probably having been entrapped into plotting with the Earl of Warwick.

Warham, William, Archbishop of Canterbury (1450 - 1532) As a member of Henry's Council, Warham promoted the more cautious, less militaristic policies of Henry VII. He was appointed as one of Katharine's Counsel during the annulment, but was not of much help to her. He put up mild resistance to Henry's first claims to be head of the Church, but died before being put to the final test.

Warner, Sir Edward (1511 - 1565) A junior member of the Royal Household, Warner had a post in the Court of Augmentations, in charge of the distribution of the wealth of the monasteries. Like others, Warner did extremely well out of the position. He served in Henry VIII's Scottish wars and became Lieutenant of the Tower. A supporter of Lady Jane Grey, and later of Wyatt's rebellion, he was pardoned, although he lost his position. Reappointed as Lieutenant under Elizabeth I, he angered the queen by allowing Lady Katherine Grey to see her husband, against orders.

Waterhouse, Sir Edward (1535 - 1591) Waterhouse was secretary to Sir Henry Sidney, Lord President of the Council of Wales and Lord Lieutenant of Ireland, and then to Walter Devereux, 1st Earl of Essex, also Lord Lieutenant. Waterhouse acquired property in Ireland and became its Chancellor of the Exchequer. He was knighted in 1584

Wharton, Thomas, 2nd Baron Wharton (1520 - 1572) Wharton joined the household of Sir Anthony Browne, and continued the family tradition of fighting the Scots. A staunch Catholic, and supporter of Mary I, on her accession, he was appointed to the Privy Council, and was Master of the Henchman. He lost favour under Elizabeth I and was imprisoned for hearing the Catholic Mass.

Whitgift, John, Archbishop of Canterbury (c. 1530 - 1604) Whitgift was ordained aged thirty, and became a royal chaplain. His moderate Protestant views accorded well with those of Elizabeth I, and he was less conciliating to the Puritans than his predecessor, Grindal. He established a school and a hospital near the archiepiscopal palace in Croydon.

Whitaker, William (c. 1547 - 1595) A graduate of Cambridge and a leading theologian in the Elizabethan church, Whitaker was strongly influenced by the doctrines of Calvin and drafted the Lambeth Articles in favour of the doctrine of predestination. His most famous work was *Disputatio de Sacra Scriptura* (1588) refuting the theology of the Counter-Reformation.

Willes, Richard (1546 - 1579?) A poet and a geographer, Willes was educated at Winchester College and New College, Oxford, before he travelled abroad to Louvain, Mainz and Trier. His volume of academic Latin verse, *Poematum liber* (1573) was dedicated to William Cecil, Lord Burghley and a later work, the *History of Travayle* (1577) was dedicated to Bridget, Countess of Bedford.

Willoughby, Katherine, 12th Baroness Willoughby d'Eresby (1519 - 1580) Daughter of William Willoughby and Maria de Salinas, long-serving lady-in-waiting to Katharine of Aragon, she was Baroness Willoughby in her own right. Katherine became the fourth wife of Charles Brandon, 1st Duke of Suffolk. Following his death, she married Richard Bertie, a member of her household.

Wolsey, Thomas, Cardinal and Archbishop of York (1473 - 1530) Wolsey rose from humble beginnings in Ipswich to be the most powerful man in England, after the king. In his early career, he was schoolmaster to the sons of the Marquis of Dorset, then a chaplain to Archbishop Deane. On Henry VIII's accession, he rapidly became indispensable, only falling from power when he failed to secure an annulment of Henry's marriage to Katharine of Aragon.

Woodville, Anne, Viscountess Bourchier (c. 1438 - 1489) Daughter of Jacquetta, Dowager Duchess of Bedford, and Sir Richard Woodville, Anne was the sister of Elizabeth Woodville. She was married to William, Viscount Bourchier, the cousin of Edward IV, as part of a wider plan to boost the Woodvilles, and provide a counterbalance to the king's Neville relatives.

Wotton, Edward (1492 - 1555) A graduate of Oxford, Wotton made a scientific study of animals, separating those which existed only in myth, from those which could be confirmed by evidence. He published his findings in *De differentiis animalium libri decem* ('Ten Books on Different Animals'), dedicated to Edward VI. A physician and graduate of Padua, he was a Fellow of the Royal College of Physicians and treated both Margaret, Countess of Salisbury, and Thomas, Duke of Norfolk.

Wright, Edward (1561 - 1615)
Wright was a mathematician and cartographer, whose treatise *Certaine Errors in Navigation,* created mathematical tables for calculating the necessary adjustments to a ship's position when using charts based on Mercator Projections, which distorts the relative sizes of landmasses.

Wriothesley, Thomas, 1st Earl of Southampton (1505 - 1550) Wriothesley began his royal service in the household of Cardinal Wolsey, where he became acquainted with Thomas Cromwell and Stephen Gardiner. Wriothesley became Cromwell's close associate, and benefited extensively from the Dissolution of the Monasteries. Later associated with the Catholic party at court, he became Lord Chancellor, and personally racked the Protestant martyr, Anne Askew. He was a Privy Councillor in Edward's reign.

Wyatt, Sir Thomas the Elder (1503 - 1542) A childhood friend of the Boleyn family, Wyatt was brought up at Allingham Castle, not far from Hever. Wyatt the Elder introduced the Petrarchan sonnet into English, and wrote some of the most famous poetry of Henry VIII's reign. He was believed to have been in love with Anne Boleyn in the 1520s, and various of his sonnets seem to allude to her. Briefly imprisoned at the time of her downfall, his friendship with Cromwell probably saved him.

Wyatt, Thomas the Younger (1521 - 1554) Son of the poet, Wyatt the Younger was a firm Protestant and led a rebellion against Mary I. His stated aim was to prevent the queen's marriage to Philip of Spain, but Mary and her government believed he planned to overthrow the queen and replace her with her half-sister, Elizabeth. Wyatt was executed, having exonerated Elizabeth of any involvement.

INDEX OF EVENTS AND ENTRIES
in order of appearance

January

The first Parliament of Henry VIII was summoned in October 1509, and began sitting on 21 January 1510, with Sir Thomas Englefield as Speaker. It was dissolved on 23 February. The main business was revenues for the crown, the confirmation of Katharine of Aragon's jointure, and the abolition of fees payable to coroners, as they were causing bodies to *'lie long unburied'*.

Henry VII commissioned a chapel to be dedicated to the Virgin Mary at Westminster Abbey. The architecture was in the late Perpendicular Gothic style, with the foundation stone laid on 24th January 1503, and the consecration taking place on 19th February 1516. Henry intended it as a mausoleum for his family, beginning with his grandmother, Katherine of Valois. It is dominated by the superb bronze tomb commissioned from Pietro Torregiano for Henry and his wife, Elizabeth of York.

Thomas Howard, 4th Duke of Norfolk, was degraded from Order of the Garter for his involvement in the Ridolfi Plot, which sought to put Mary, Queen of Scots on the English throne, with Norfolk as her consort.

February

The most violent and bloody of all Shakespeare's plays, *Titus Andronicus*, centres on revenge. The title character returns from ten years at war, and the loss of 21 sons in battle, to find himself betrayed at home. He has brought his captive, Tamora, the Queen of the Goths with him, having sacrificed her eldest son. Tamora becomes Empress, and wreaks bloody revenge, which Titus repays.

The Battle of Ancrum Moor, fought between Scotland and England as part of the War of the Rough Wooing, was a victory for Scotland. Although it halted the English temporarily, and resulted in the return to their natural loyalty of some Scottish lords who had defected to England, the victory was short-lived.

March

Founded in 1517 by Richard Foxe, Bishop of Winchester, Corpus Christi College, Oxford, has specialised in the study of classics from its earliest days. Cardinal Reginald Pole was a fellow in the 1520s, and the Spanish humanist, Juan Luis Vives, taught there during the same decade.

Waltham Abbey was the last religious community to be closed during the Dissolution of the Monasteries ordered by Henry VIII in the 1530s. The abbot, Robert, and his officers were all granted comfortable pensions, and it was mooted that Waltham, which had been the richest house in Essex, should be re-founded as a cathedral. Many of the vestments were given to local parish churches, and the majority of the plate and jewels went to the king. A proportion of the lands were granted to Sir Anthony Denny.

Elizabeth I granted Letters Patent to her *'trusty and well-beloved servant,'* Walter Raleigh to *'find out and view…remote countries…not actually possessed of any Christian Prince'* and to hold them forever, under her authority.

May

Cardinal Wolsey supervised mass burning of Lutheran books at St Paul's Cathedral in response to Pope Leo X's bull, *Exsurge Domine* of 1520, which required the clergy to search out his heretical works and burn them in public.

At the Battle of Langside, Mary, Queen of Scots sought to reimpose her authority, after escaping imprisonment in Lochleven Castle, where she had been forced to abdicate. Despite having superior numbers, her army was defeated. Mary escaped the field, and chose to travel to England in hopes of gaining Elizabeth I's support. Help was not forthcoming, and Mary spent the rest of her life as a prisoner.

The sending of the Spanish Armada was an act of open warfare after years of skirmishing between England and Spain. The English feared that Spain would invade to reimpose Catholicism, whilst the Spanish resented English interference on behalf of Protestant insurgents in The Netherlands, and the constant attacks on its fleets bringing silver from the Americas. The Spanish Armada attack of 1588, although the most famous, was not the last.

June

As part of the ongoing war with Spain, Elizabeth I reluctantly granted permission for a pre-emptive strike against a new Spanish armada, arming in Cadiz. The Earl of Essex led an Anglo-Dutch fleet with a view to taking the ships, and intercepting the Spanish fleet returning from the Americas, laden with silver. The Spanish fired their own fleet to prevent capture, and the Anglo-Dutch forces sacked and burnt the city, but failed to take the treasure fleet.

The first St Paul's was consecrated in AD604, followed by two later buildings. That known in the Tudor period was the stone building consecrated in 1148 and completed in 1240. The lightning of 1561 enveloped the tower and roof in flame, and the cathedral was extensively damaged. Initial plans to rebuild in 1633 were shelved, and during the Civil War it suffered further depredation, before being replaced by Christopher Wren's Baroque masterpiece.

Tottel's Miscellany, correctly named *Songes and Sonettes Written By the Ryght Honorable Lord Henry Howard, late Earle of Surrey*, Thomas Wyatt the Elder and others contained 271 different entries, including 54 sonnets, mainly dating from the 1530s and 1540s when Wyatt and Surrey flourished at the court of Henry VIII.

The Field of Cloth of Gold in 1520 was one of the most extravagant displays of national pride and ostentation disguised as diplomacy, of the sixteenth century. Henry VIII and François I met, alongside their queens and courtiers, and feasted, jousted, wrestled and danced both literally and metaphorically for nearly two weeks. Within two years, the countries were again at war.

In 1502, Henry VII of England signed two treaties with the Holy Roman Emperor Maximilian – one related to trade, and the other was an agreement not to harbour each other's rebels. Henry was hoping to minimise the danger of Edmund de la Pole, the 'White Rose' attracting the support that the pretender, Perkin Warbeck, had.

In 1549, a new form of church service was developed, by Archbishop Thomas Cranmer. Although based on the old Latin Use of Sarum, it leant towards Protestantism, although not enough to satisfy the more radical Reformers. This Book of Common Prayer, as it was known, was superseded in 1552 by a more Protestant version.

The *Henry Grâce à Dieu* was Henry VIII's largest ship; laid down at Woolwich in 1512, she was completed after two years, and measured 50m in length, and carried a crew of up to 1,000. She carried 43 heavy guns (including 20 of bronze) and 151 lighter ones. In the 1530s, she was reduced in weight. Crew numbers fell to 700 and only 151 guns in total were carried.

Following the assassination of her husband, Henry Stuart, Lord Darnley, Mary Queen of Scots married the Earl of Bothwell. Whether or not she was implicated in Darnley's death

remains hotly debated, but a significant proportion of the Scottish nobles rose up against her. The two sides met at Carberry Hill. Mary surrendered without a fight, believing that, if Bothwell were exiled her authority would be maintained. She was mistaken, and, after public humiliation, was sent a captive to Lochleven Castle.

The Battle of Stoke was the last pitched battle in the Wars of the Roses. A Yorkist army, led by John de la Pole, Earl of Lincoln, and Viscount Lovell fought Henry VII's army at Stoke. The figurehead of the Yorkists was a young boy named Lambert Simnel, who had been claimed to be Edward, Earl of Warwick, and crowned as Edward VI in Dublin.

Jesus College, Oxford, was founded to provide education for clerics in the nascent Church of England. The majority of the eight original benefactors, probably led by Dr Hugh ap Rice, Treasurer of St David's, were either Welsh or held Welsh livings, and the college continued to attract mainly Welsh students and principals well into the twentieth century. It still has a strong Welsh connection.

July

On the death of James V of Scotland, his week-old daughter, Mary, became queen. Immediately, her great-uncle, Henry VIII of England, saw an opportunity to impose English control of Scotland. He persuaded the Scots regent, the Earl of Arran, to agree that Mary would marry Henry's son, Edward. The Treaty of Greenwich, agreeing the terms was signed by Henry VIII and Arran, but was rejected by the Scottish Parliament.

The League of Venice was created to counter the advance of the French into Italy under Charles VIII. Charles had been offered the throne of Naples by Pope Innocent VIII, and in 1492, encouraged by the Duke of Milan, Charles marched through the peninsula at the head of army, and entered Naples. The other Italian states, the Emperor and the new pope, Alexander VI, became alarmed at the potential for French dominance of Italy and banded together in the League to oust him. The ensuing conflicts lasted until 1559.

By 1545, England and France had been at war for a year. Henry had captured Boulogne, and the French now sought revenge by sending a fleet to attack the coastal towns of England. In what became known as the Battle of the Solent, the two navies attacked each other from a distance, with little damage done. The *Mary Rose* heeled and sank – for reasons that are still not certain. The French claimed a hit, whilst the English said that a sudden wind change took water into an overburdened vessel.

During the Anglo-French war of 1543 – 1545, Henry VIII captured Boulogne, and the French retaliated by landing forces on the Isle of Wight. Whilst the details are uncertain, the French were unable to take effective control of any of the island's ports and retreated.

August

In 1513, Henry VIII allied with his father-in-law, Ferdinand of Aragon, and the Holy Roman Emperor, Maximilian, to invade France. Thanks to the brilliant administrative ability of Cardinal Wolsey, Henry's army was well-disciplined and well-provisioned. They besieged the town of Thérouanne. The French hoped to raise the siege, but, caught in an exposed position, the small French cavalry force was put to flight by the Anglo-Imperial force – the name of Battle of the Spurs refers to the speed of the French retreat. Several valuable hostages were taken and Thérouanne and Tournai captured.

In early August 1485, Henry Tudor, Earl of Richmond, landed with a small force of Lancastrians, disaffected Yorkists and French and Breton mercenaries in South Wales. He marched through Wales and the West Midlands of England, gathering support as he went, to confront Richard III in a field near Market Bosworth. Henry had the victory, Richard was killed, and thus the Battle of Bosworth inaugurated 128 years of Tudor rule.

In 1513, with England at war with France, James IV of Scotland, the ally of Louis XII of France, but also Henry VIII's brother-in-law, was torn between his two alliances. Eventually, he decided that he must support France, and raised a massive army to invade England, whilst Henry VIII and the majority of his army were in France. Katharine of Aragon, as Regent, reacted to the Scottish threat by confiscating all lands held by Scots, and requiring them to leave the country. Meanwhile, working with the queen, the Earl of Surrey mustered an army and marched north.

September

In early September, James IV of Scotland and his army of some 42,000 men crossed into England. They took the castles of Norham, Wark, Etal and Ford, then drew up in a commanding position. The English commander, Surrey, came around behind the Scots army, and James moved from his advantageous location. The resulting Battle of Flodden was a savage and disorganised slaughter. The Scots were decimated, and James was killed.

The Battle of Pinkie Cleugh was the last pitched battle between England and Scotland before the Union of the Crowns. The English government sought to force a match between Mary, Queen of Scots and Edward VI of England, to bring the two countries under English control. The English, despite their victory, did not have sufficient manpower or money to follow up the battle with permanent occupation.

November

When James VI of Scotland became James I of England, many English Catholics hoped that the penal laws against them would be relaxed. James, however, whilst he was not interested in delving into the beliefs of his subjects, and had known Catholics amongst his ministers, was not prepared to change the law. Frustrated, a group of young, Catholic gentlemen came up with a conspiracy, known as the Gunpowder Plot, to blow up Parliament, and place James' daughter, Elizabeth, on the throne as a puppet queen. One of plotters sent a warning to a Catholic lord not to attend Parliament, a search was made and Guy Fawkes and the gunpowder were discovered.

The first Oxford University library dated to the 1320s. It was greatly enhanced by the gift of 281 volumes by Humphrey, Duke of Gloucester, brother of Henry V, and housed in a new building. During the Reformation, the Dean of Christ Church, keen to purge the university of any remnants of Catholic 'superstition', burnt some of the books, and dispersed the others. In the 1590s, the wealthy Thomas Bodley refurbished Duke Humphrey's library and filled it with a collection of some 2,500 books.

In 1553, Edward VI wrote his *Devise for the Succession* in which he tried to pass the throne to his Protestant cousin, Lady Jane Grey, rather than his Catholic half-sister, Mary. On the king's death, Jane's father-in-law, the Duke of Northumberland, and her father, the Duke of Suffolk, tried to put the *Devise* into effect. They failed, and Mary triumphed. Jane and her husband were tried at the Guildhall and convicted, but Mary had no desire to punish them, seeing them as victims of their fathers' ambition. It was not until Suffolk became embroiled in another rebellion that Jane and Guilford were executed.

In 1542 war broke out once again between England and Scotland. The relationship between Henry VIII and his nephew, James V, had never been good, and James's failure to meet Henry at York, as Henry believed had been promised, was an insult the English king could not forgive. The Scots scored a notable victory at Haddon Rigg, but then lost heavily at Solway Moss, with a number of the Scots lords being captured and taken to London. James did not fight himself, but died within a fortnight.

December

Charles Brandon was the son of Sir William Brandon, Henry VII's standard-bearer killed at the Battle of Bosworth. The orphaned Charles was brought up in and around the court, and became Henry VIII's closest friend. As a mark of favour, Brandon was given the wardship and marriage of Elizabeth, Viscountess Lisle. He decided to marry her himself and Henry allowed him to use her title. Soon, a greater prize, Henry's sister, Mary, Dowager Queen of France, appeared, and Brandon married her. It was some time before he could be persuaded to relinquish Elizabeth's title or goods.

In 1563, Drake sailed to the Americas for the first time, with his cousin, Sir John Hawkins. Piracy and plundering of Spanish or Portuguese ships and colonies was considered an intrinsic part of exploration, and Drake excelled in it. Following an exceptionally successful raid on the Spanish Main in 1573, Elizabeth I was impressed with his exploits and commissioned Drake to undertake another expedition in 1577. Captaining the *Pelican*, with four other ships in the fleet, Drake led a truly swash-buckling expedition, circumnavigating the globe, and arriving back in England in September 1580.

With the expansion of sea-trade and the improved opportunities for trading with the East, by the end of the sixteenth century, London merchants were expanding their horizons. In late 1600 the Honourable Company of Merchants of London Trading into the East Indies was instituted. Led by Sir Thomas Smythe, they petitioned Elizabeth I, who granted them a charter.

Tudor Book of Days
Published in Great Britain in 2017 by
Graffeg Limited

Written by Tudor Times
Designed and produced by Graffeg Limited
copyright © 2017

Graffeg Limited, 24 Stradey Park Business
Centre, Mwrwg Road, Llangennech,
Llanelli, Carmarthenshire SA14 8YP Wales
UK Tel 01554 824000 www.graffeg.com

Cover image: Tudor roses and flowers
embroidered on a Chasuble. England,
mid 16th century. © V&A Images /
Alamy Stock Photo.

ISBN 9781912213238

1 2 3 4 5 6 7 8 9